The Consumer Credit and Sales
Legal Practice Series

AUTOMOBILE FRAUD

Odometer, Salvage, and Lemon Laundering Fraud,
Title Abuses and Yo-Yo Sales

2013 Supplement

Keyword Search Entire Book

Go to
www.nclc.org/books

See *page ix* for details.

Carolyn L. Carter
John W. Van Alst
Jonathan Sheldon

National Consumer Law Center®
7 Winthrop Square, 4th Floor   Boston, MA 02110   www.nclc.org

About NCLC®

The National Consumer Law Center®, a nonprofit corporation founded in 1969, assists consumers, advocates, and public policy makers nationwide who use the powerful and complex tools of consumer law to ensure justice and fair treatment for all, particularly those whose poverty renders them powerless to demand accountability from the economic marketplace. For more information, go to www.nclc.org.

Ordering NCLC Publications

Order securely online at www.nclc.org, or contact Publications Department, National Consumer Law Center, 7 Winthrop Square, 4th Floor, Boston, MA 02110, (617) 542-9595, FAX: (617) 542-8028, e-mail: publications@nclc.org.

Training and Conferences

NCLC participates in numerous national, regional, and local consumer law trainings. Its annual fall conference is a forum for consumer rights attorneys from legal services programs, private practice, government, and nonprofit organizations to share insights into common problems and explore novel and tested approaches that promote consumer justice in the marketplace. Contact NCLC for more information or see our website.

Case Consulting

Case analysis, consulting and co-counseling for lawyers representing vulnerable consumers are among NCLC's important activities. Administration on Aging funds allow us to provide free consulting to legal services advocates representing elderly consumers on many types of cases. Massachusetts Legal Assistance Corporation funds permit case assistance to advocates representing low-income Massachusetts consumers. Other funding may allow NCLC to provide very brief consultations to other advocates without charge. More comprehensive case analysis and research is available for a reasonable fee. See our website for more information at www.nclc.org.

Charitable Donations and Cy Pres *Awards*

NCLC's work depends in part on the support of private donors. Tax-deductible donations should be made payable to National Consumer Law Center, Inc. For more information, contact Gerald Tuckman of NCLC's Development Office at (617) 542-8010 or gtuckman@nclc.org. NCLC has also received generous court-approved *cy pres* awards arising from consumer class actions to advance the interests of class members. For more information, contact Robert Hobbs (rhobbs@nclc.org) or Rich Dubois (rdubois@nclc.org) at (617) 542-8010.

Comments and Corrections

Write to the above address to the attention of the Editorial Department or e-mail consumerlaw@nclc.org.

About This Volume

This is the 2013 Supplement to *Automobile Fraud* (4th ed. 2011). Retain the 2011 Fourth Edition and this Supplement; discard prior editions and supplements. This book includes a companion website. Continuing developments can be found in periodic supplements to and revised editions of this volume, on the companion website, and in NCLC eReports.

Cite This Volume As

National Consumer Law Center, Automobile Fraud (4th ed. 2011 and Supp.).

About the Authors

Carolyn L. Carter is NCLC's deputy director for advocacy and was formerly co-director of Legal Services, Inc., in Gettysburg, Pennsylvania and director of the Law Reform Office of the Cleveland Legal Aid Society. She is the editor of *Pennsylvania Consumer Law*, editor of the first edition of *Ohio Consumer Law*, author of *Repossessions,* co-author of *Consumer Credit Regulation, Mortgage Lending, Consumer Warranty Law, Collection Actions,* and *Unfair and Deceptive Acts and Practices,* and contributing author to other NCLC publications. She was the 1992 recipient of the Vern Countryman Consumer Law Award.

John W. Van Alst is an NCLC staff attorney whose focus includes deceptive practices law, automobile fraud, and manufactured home issues. He formerly was an attorney at Legal Aid of North Carolina for seven years, where he handled a broad range of consumer issues, and was also an adjunct clinical professor at the University of North Carolina School of Law. He is co-author of *Consumer Warranty Law* and *Consumer Rights for Domestic Violence Survivors.* He is a contributing author to *Consumer Credit Regulation, Mortgage Lending, Unfair and Deceptive Acts and Practices, Foreclosures,* and *Repossessions.*

Jonathan Sheldon has been an NCLC staff attorney writing and consulting on automobile fraud, deceptive practices law and other consumer law topics since 1976. Previously he was a staff attorney with the Federal Trade Commission. His publications include *Unfair and Deceptive Acts and Practices, Federal Deception Law, Consumer Warranty Law, Consumer Arbitration Agreements, Consumer Credit Regulation,* and *Collection Actions.*

Acknowledgments

Special thanks to Emily Green Caplan for work on Chapter 6; Eric Secoy for editorial supervision; Kim Calvi for editorial assistance; Kurt Terwilliger and Shirlron Williams for assistance checking the citations; Shannon Halbrook and Microsearch for designing and implementing the companion website; and Xylutions for typesetting services.

What Your Library Should Contain

The Consumer Credit and Sales Legal Practice Series contains 20 titles, updated annually, arranged into four libraries, and designed to be an attorney's primary practice guide and legal resource in all 50 states. Titles are available individually or as part of the complete 20-volume series. Each title includes free access to a companion website containing sample pleadings, primary sources, and other practice aids, allowing pinpoint searches and the pasting of text into a word processor. Access remains free as long as purchasers keep their titles current.

Debtor Rights Library

2012 Tenth Edition (Two Volumes) and Companion Website

Consumer Bankruptcy Law and Practice: the definitive personal bankruptcy manual, from the initial interview to final discharge, including consumer rights when a company files for bankruptcy. This practice package contains the leading expert analysis of individual bankruptcy law and such practice aids as over 150 pleadings and forms, a client questionnaire and handout, the latest Bankruptcy Code, Rules, and fee schedules, a date calculator, and means test data.

2011 Seventh Edition (Two Volumes), 2013 Supplement, and Companion Website

Fair Debt Collection: the basic reference covering the Fair Debt Collection Practices Act and common law, state statutory and other federal debt collection protections. Thousands of unique case summaries cover reported and unreported FDCPA cases by category. The companion website contains sample pleadings and discovery, the FTC Commentary, an index to and the full text of *all* FTC staff opinion letters, and other practice aids.

2012 Fourth Edition, 2013 Supplement, and Companion Website

Foreclosures: examines RESPA and other federal and state requirements placed on mortgage loan servicers, including the new CFPB regulations, and details on loan modification and mediation programs implemented by federal and state governments. The volume features standing and substantive and procedural defenses to foreclosure and tactics after the foreclosure sale. Special chapters cover tax liens, land installment sales contracts, manufactured home and condominium foreclosures, and other topics.

2010 Seventh Edition, 2012 Supplement, and Companion Website

Repossessions: a unique guide to motor vehicle and mobile home repossessions, threatened seizures of household goods, statutory liens, and automobile lease and rent-to-own default remedies. The volume examines UCC Article 9 and hundreds of other federal and state statutes regulating repossessions.

2010 Fourth Edition, 2012 Supplement and Companion Website

Student Loan Law: collection harassment; closed school, disability, and other discharges; tax intercepts, wage garnishment, and offset of social security benefits; and repayment plans, consolidation loans, deferments, private student loans, and non-payment of loan based on school fraud.

2011 Fifth Edition and Companion Website

Access to Utility Service: consumer rights as to regulated and unregulated utilities, including telecommunications, terminations, billing errors, low-income payment plans, utility allowances in subsidized housing, LIHEAP, and weatherization.

Credit and Banking Library

2012 Eighth Edition (Two Volumes) and Companion Website

Truth in Lending: detailed analysis of *all* aspects of TILA, the Consumer Leasing Act, the Fair Credit Billing Act, the Home Ownership and Equity Protection Act (HOEPA), and the Credit CARD Act, including the major 2010 amendments. Appendices and the website contain the Acts, Reg. Z, Reg. M, and their official staff commentaries, numerous sample pleadings, rescission notices, two programs to compute APRs, TIL legislative history, and a unique compilation of *all Federal Register* notices and supplementary information on Regulation Z since 1969. The text references to both FRB and CFPB versions of Regulation Z.

2010 Seventh Edition, 2012 Supplement, and Companion Website

Fair Credit Reporting: the key resource for handling any type of credit reporting issue, from cleaning up blemished credit records to suing reporting agencies and creditors for inaccurate reports. Covers the new FACTA changes, identity theft, creditor liability for failing to properly reinvestigate disputed information, credit scoring, privacy issues, the Credit Repair Organizations Act, state credit reporting and repair statutes, and common law claims.

Superseded

The Cost of Credit is replaced by two new titles, *Mortgage Lending* and *Consumer Credit Regulation*. Responding to major changes in the nature and regulation of mortgage lending and other consumer credit, these two new titles expand upon, update, and re-organize *The Cost of Credit* material.

2012 First Edition, 2013 Supplement, and Companion Website, replacing The Cost of Credit

Mortgage Lending: covers federal and state regulation (and federal preemption) of the origination and the terms of mortgage loans, including ability to pay, steering, churning, flipping, appraisals, loan broker compensation, insurance, adjustable rates, negative amortization, interest rate limitations, late fees, reverse mortgages, holder-in-due course, mortgage litigation, and claims against failed banks.

2012 First Edition, 2013 Supplement, and Companion Website, replacing The Cost of Credit

Consumer Credit Regulation: examines federal and state regulation (and federal preemption of state regulation) concerning credit cards, payday loans, automobile finance and installment sales, auto title pawns, rent-to-own, refund anticipation loans, "sale" of the consumer's future income stream and other non-mortgage lending. Special chapters on credit math, what is interest, and credit insurance.

2013 Fifth Edition and Companion Website

Consumer Banking and Payments Law: covers checks, telechecks, electronic fund transfers, electronic check conversions, money orders, and debit, payroll, unemployment, and other prepaid cards. The title also covers new federal regulations on remittances, banker's right of setoff, electronic transfers of federal and state benefit payments, and a special chapter on electronic records and signatures.

2013 Sixth Edition and Companion Website

Credit Discrimination: analysis of the Equal Credit Opportunity Act, Fair Housing Act, Civil Rights Acts, and state credit discrimination statutes, including reprints of all relevant federal interpretations, government enforcement actions, and numerous sample pleadings.

Consumer Litigation Library

2011 Second Edition, 2013 Supplement, and Companion Website

Collection Actions: a complete guide to consumer defenses and counterclaims to collection lawsuits filed in court or in arbitration, with extensive discussion of setting aside default judgments and limitations on a collector's post-judgment remedies. Special chapters include the rights of active duty military, and unique issues involving medical debt, government collections, collector's attorney fees, and bad check laws.

2011 Sixth Edition, 2012 Supplement, and Companion Website

Consumer Arbitration Agreements: successful approaches to challenge arbitration agreements' enforceability and waivers of class arbitration, the interrelation of the Federal Arbitration Act and state law, class actions and punitive damages in arbitration, implications of NAF's withdrawal from consumer arbitrations, the right to discovery, import of recent Supreme Court rulings, and other topics.

2013 Eighth Edition and Companion Website

Consumer Class Actions: makes class litigation manageable even for small offices, including numerous sample pleadings, class certification memoranda, discovery, class notices, settlement materials, and much more on the companion website. Includes a detailed analysis of the Class Action Fairness Act, state class action rules and case law, and other topics.

Website and 2012 Index Guide: ALL pleadings from ALL NCLC treatises, including Consumer Law Pleadings Numbers One through Eighteen

Consumer Law Pleadings: over *2000* notable pleadings from all types of consumer cases, including predatory lending, foreclosures, automobile fraud, lemon laws, debt collection, fair credit reporting, home improvement fraud, student loans, and lender liability. Finding aids pinpoint desired pleading in seconds, ready to paste into a word processor.

Deception and Warranties Library

2012 Eighth Edition and Companion Website

Unfair and Deceptive Acts and Practices: the only practice manual covering all aspects of a deceptive practices case in every state. Citations to tens of thousands of state UDAP and FTC cases. Special sections on automobile sales, unfair insurance practices, unfair and deceptive credit practices, third party liability, attorney fees, and many other topics.

2011 Fourth Edition, 2013 Supplement, and Companion Website

Automobile Fraud: examination of title law, "yo-yo" sales, odometer tampering, lemon laundering, sale of salvage and wrecked cars, undisclosed prior use, and prior damage to new cars. The website contains numerous sample pleadings and title search techniques.

2010 Fourth Edition, 2013 Supplement, and Companion Website

Consumer Warranty Law: comprehensive treatment of new and used car lemon laws, the Magnuson-Moss Warranty Act, UCC Articles 2 and 2A, mobile home, new home, and assistive device warranty laws, FTC Used Car Rule, tort theories, car repair and home improvement statutes, service contract and lease laws, with numerous sample pleadings.

2012 First Edition and Companion Website

Federal Deception Law: new treatise covering FTC and CFPB rulemaking, special chapters on the FTC Holder and Telemarketing Sales Rules, federal restrictions on unwanted calls and texts, junk faxes and spam, federal and state RICO, the federal False Claims Act, federal and state regulation of debt relief services, and more.

NCLC's Companion Websites

Every NCLC manual includes a companion website, allowing rapid access to appendices, pleadings, primary sources, and other practice aids. Search for documents by category or with a table of contents or various keyword search options. All documents can be downloaded, printed, and copy-pasted into a word processing document. Pleadings are also available in Word format. Web access is free with each title ordered and remains free as long as a title is kept current.

Website continually subject to update

Consumer Law on the Web: combines *everything* from the 20 other NCLC companion websites. Using *Consumer Law on the Web*, instead of multiple individual companion websites, is often the fastest and most convenient way to pinpoint and retrieve key documents among the thousands available on our individual companion websites.

Other NCLC Publications for Lawyers

Over 100 articles a year

NCLC eReports: a web-based newsletter (currently free to those on automatic subscription to updates to NCLC treatises) containing over 100 articles a year, with the latest consumer law developments, novel ideas, innovative tactics, and key insights from NCLC's experienced consumer law attorneys. Articles can be copy-pasted into a word processor, web links are live, and past articles are easily searchable. Optional free e-mail alerts announce new articles and list the latest new regulations, statutes, and key court decisions.

About the Companion Website and Other Online Resources

> Visit **www.nclc.org/books** for links to all the book-related online resources listed below, including the treatises' companion websites, *NCLC eReports*, a search engine to search the full text of all treatises, the Quick Reference, and our online bookstore.

The Companion Websites: www.nclc.org/webaccess

Purchase of any title in NCLC's consumer law practice series includes free access to its companion website. Access remains free if you subscribe or continue to purchase updates to that title. Frequently updated, NCLC companion websites offer the treatises' appendices plus hundreds of additional documents in PDF and Microsoft Word formats—pleadings, forms, statutes, regulations, agency interpretations, legislative and regulatory history, and much more—all easily located with flexible, powerful search tools. The sites can be easily viewed on a smartphone or tablet, and documents can be electronically searched, printed, downloaded, and copy-pasted into a word processor.

In addition to the current federal statutes and regulations relating to automobile fraud, the companion website to *Automobile Fraud* contains the federal Odometer Act prior to re-codification, key supplemental information to NHTSA regulations, summaries of state automobile fraud legislation, and NHTSA letters interpreting odometer requirements. Of particular note are over 100 sample pleadings for automobile fraud cases, including complaints, discovery requests, deposition transcripts, pre-trial motions, voir dire, opening statements, expert reports, closing statements, jury instructions, and attorney fee documents.

The website also has a number of tools to simplify title search requests, including applicable request forms from the 50 states, links to state titling offices, and sample reports from Carfax and other companies offering summary vehicle information.

We highly recommend reading the Help page on the website, found at the top of the left toolbar once you are logged in.

Registering for the Companion Website

One-time registration is required to access the companion website. Once registered, a user subsequently logging in will be granted immediate access to all the companion websites he or she is authorized to use.

To register for the first time, go to **www.nclc.org/webaccess** and click "Register as a New User." Enter the Companion Website Registration Number[1] found on the packing statement or invoice accompanying this book. Then enter the requested information to create your account. An e-mail address may be used for the username, or a different username may be chosen.

Users do *not* need to register more than once.[2] If you subsequently purchase additional NCLC titles, you will automatically be given access to the corresponding companion websites. Registering a second time with the same registration number overrides a prior username and password.

Once registered, go to www.nclc.org/webaccess, enter your username and password, and click the Login button. Then select a companion website from the list.

An alternative log-in method may be particularly useful for libraries, legal aid offices, or law firms that subscribe to the entire set of NCLC treatises. Simply send an e-mail to publications@nclc.org with a list or range of static IP addresses for which access should be permitted. Users from those addresses can then go to **www.nclc.org/ipaccess** to be granted access *without* entering a username and password.

Once logged in, users can click the Preferences link located on the top toolbar to change their account information.

Locating Documents on the Companion Website

The companion website provides three ways to locate documents:

1. The search page (the home page) uses keyword searches to find documents—full text searches of all documents on the website or searches of just the documents' titles. Enter text in the appropriate field and click the Search button.

- Narrow the search to documents of a certain type (for example, federal regulations or pleadings) by making a

---

1 If you cannot locate this number, contact NCLC Publications at (617) 542-9595 or publications@nclc.org.

2 If you have not updated *any* of your NCLC treatises for some time, your account may be deleted; if this happens, you must re-register if you subsequently purchase a book.

selection from the "Document Type" menu, and then perform a full text or document title search.

- To locate a specific appendix section, select the appendix section number (for example, A.2.3) or a partial identifier (for example, A) in the search page's "Appendix" drop-down fields.
- When searching documents' full text, each entry in your search results will include excerpts of the document, showing your search terms highlighted in context.
- Click on the "Search Hints" link for a quick reference to special search operators, wildcards, shortcuts, and complex searches. Read this information closely, as syntax and search operators may be slightly different from those used by other search engines.

2. The contents page (click the "Contents" tab at the top of the page) is a traditional nested table of contents. Click a branch to expand it into a list of sub-branches or documents. Each document appears once in this contents tree.

3. The pleading finder page (click the "Pleading Finder" link at the top of the search page, if available) allows pleadings to be located using one or more menus, such as "Type of Pleading" or "Subject." **Select more than one item from a menu, or deselect items, by holding the Ctrl key while clicking.** For example, make one selection from "Type of Pleading–General," one from "Subject," and three from "Legal Claims" to locate all pleadings of that type and subject that contain one or more of the three legal claims selected. If this search produces insufficient results, simply broaden the search by deselecting "Subject" and/or "Legal Claims" to find pleadings of that type in any subject area or based upon any legal claim. This page also includes optional fields to specify terms to be found in the documents' text or titles, to further narrow search results.

Over 2000 pleadings are also available at NCLC's *Consumer Law Pleadings* website using the same search techniques discussed above. Pleadings can also be located using *Consumer Law Pleadings'* index guide, which lists pleadings organized by type, subject area, legal claim, title, and other categories identical to those on the website.

How to Use the Documents, Find Microsoft Word Versions, and Locate Additional Features

Click a document title in your search results or on the contents page to view the document in your web browser. Text may be copy-pasted directly from the page or the full document may be downloaded as a PDF file for easier printing. (You will need a PDF reader to open PDF documents; the free Adobe Reader is available at www.adobe.com.) Additionally, pleadings and certain other documents can be downloaded in Microsoft Word format, enabling the opening of entire documents in a word processor. Icons to download PDF and Word versions are found at the top of the page.

Links on the left-hand toolbar bring you to credit math software, search tips, other websites, tables of contents and indices of all NCLC treatises, and other practice aids. Links to

especially important new developments will be placed toward the bottom of the "Search" page.

Search the Full Text of NCLC's Treatises: www.nclc.org/keyword

Keyword Search Entire Book 🔍

NCLC offers a handy online utility to search the full text of our publications. This **free** search utility is found at **www.nclc.org/keyword** and requires no registration or log-in. While the chapters' text is not available online, this web-based search engine will find a word or phrase, which can then easily be located in this printed treatise. Select this book, enter a search term or combination of search terms—such as a case name, a regulation citation, or other keywords—and the page numbers containing those terms will be listed. Search results are shown in context, enabling selection of the most relevant pages.

The search utility can also be used to search other NCLC publications. Simply perform the search as described above and select the publication to be searched.

NCLC eReports: *www.nclc.org/ereports*

NCLC eReports, found alongside the treatises' companion websites at **www.nclc.org/webaccess** or **www.nclc.org/ereports**, is a collection of short articles by NCLC's experts discussing recent consumer law developments. About ten new articles are published each month, with older articles available in a searchable archive. Treatise subscribers have free access to *NCLC eReports*, while others may purchase a one-year subscription. Current summaries and sample articles can be found on the NCLC online bookstore at www.nclc.org/shop. NCLC sends occasional eAlerts to inform our readers about new *eReports* articles and other news items; visit **www.nclc.org/ealerts** to sign up.

NCLC's Online Bookstore: www.nclc.org/shop

Our online bookstore at **www.nclc.org/shop** provides information about all twenty NCLC treatises and our other titles, including current tables of contents, indices, sample pages, and more. Click the "For Lawyers" link and scroll down to the book you are interested in. The PDF-format documents found there can be quickly searched for a word or phrase.

Quick Reference, a Series-Wide Index: www.nclc.org/qr

The Quick Reference, found at **www.nclc.org/qr**, is an alphabetical index spanning all twenty NCLC treatises. It lists over 1000 subjects and indicates the book(s) and section(s) where each subject is discussed.

Contents

Chapter 5

Federal and State Odometer Requirements

Chapter 6

Remedies for MVICSA and State Odometer Act Violations

Chapter 7   Other Statutes Specifically Relating to Automobile Fraud

Chapter 8   Common Law Fraud, Deceit, and Misrepresentation

Chapter 10

Litigating Automobile Fraud Cases

Appendix A   Federal Statutes

Appendix B   Federal Regulations

Appendix C   State Laws Relating to Automobile Fraud

Appendix D   **State-by-State Information on Requesting Title Histories** 55
replacement appendix

Appendix E   Sample Documents

new section

Chapter 1

Introduction and Practice Checklist

1.3 Automobile Frauds Analyzed in Other NCLC Treatises

Page 3

1.3.2 Automobile Warranties and Repairs

Replace note 3 with:

    3   National Consumer Law Center, Unfair and Deceptive Acts and Practices § 7.10 (8th ed. 2012).

1.3.3 Deceptive Pricing and Sales Techniques

Replace notes 4, 5 with:

    4   (8th ed. 2012).
    5   National Consumer Law Center, Unfair and Deceptive Acts and Practices § 7.1 (8th ed. 2012).

Page 4

1.3.4 Trade-Ins, Yo-Yo Sales, and Financing

Replace notes 9, 12 with:

    9   (8th ed. 2012).
    12   (8th ed. 2012).

1.3.5 Credit Insurance, GAP Insurance, and Service Contracts

Replace notes 14, 15, 18 with:

    14   National Consumer Law Center, Unfair and Deceptive Acts and Practices §§ 7.2.6, 7.2.7, 9.5.7 (8th ed. 2012).
    15   (8th ed. 2012).
    18   National Consumer Law Center, Unfair and Deceptive Acts and Practices § 9.5 (8th ed. 2012).

1.3.7 Leasing

Replace notes 20, 22 with:

    20   National Consumer Law Center, Truth in Lending Ch. 13 (8th ed. 2012).
    22   National Consumer Law Center, Unfair and Deceptive Acts and Practices § 7.6 (8th ed. 2012).

Page 5

1.3.10 Forced-Placed Automobile Insurance

Replace note 26 with:

    26   National Consumer Law Center, Unfair and Deceptive Acts and Practices § 9.5.10 (8th ed. 2012).

Chapter 2

Investigatory Techniques

2.3 Summary Title History

Page 32

2.3.2 Carfax

Add to text after sentence containing note 95:

Even dealers have brought actions against Carfax claiming that it reports items such as structural damage inconsistently and inaccurately.[95.1]

> 95.1   Off Lease Only, Inc. v. Carfax, Inc., 2012 WL 1966372 (S.D. Fla. May 31, 2012).

Page 33

Replace subsection's next-to-last paragraph with:

Carfax claims that it has an advantage over other vehicle history services because of proprietary information sources and because its data includes information on ownership, history, mileage accuracy, lemon and recall checks, accident checks, and safety and reliability reports.

Page 34

2.3.4 The National Motor Vehicle Title Information System

Replace subsection's second and third paragraphs with:

The regulations require all state motor vehicle departments to provide titling information to the NMVTIS database by January 1, 2010.[100] This information must be provided electronically, at least once every twenty-four hours, although some states are moving towards real time updates. As of November 2012, thirty-three states provide data and inquire into the system before issuing new titles, eight states provide data to the system but do not make inquiries before issuing new titles, and ten states (including the District of Columbia) are in development. The NMVTIS website, as of November 2012, reports that eighty-seven percent of motor vehicles in the United States are in the NMVTIS system.

As of March 31, 2009, all insurance carriers are required to report to NMVTIS monthly all junk or salvage vehicles which they have obtained in the past month that are from the current model year or any of the four prior model years, if the insurer has declared the vehicle to be a total loss.[101] Also as of March 31, 2009, all auto recyclers, salvage yards, and junk yards are required to report to NMVTIS monthly all junk or salvage vehicles which they have obtained during the past month.[102] As of 2011, over 9000 of these entities have registered to report information and 28.1 million salvage or total loss records have been added to the system.

> 100   26 C.F.R. § 25.54(a).
> 101   26 C.F.R. § 25.55(a).
> 102   26 C.F.R. § 25.56(a).

Page 36

2.3.6 Insurance Databases

Replace third sentence of subsection's final paragraph with:

The subpoena should seek any and all electronic media that NICB maintains, controls, or has access to, including but not limited to:

- Vehicle identification number (VIN);
- Manufacturer's build information;
- Date of any claim or incident involving the vehicle;
- Name, address, and phone number of any insurance company involved in any such claim;
- Information regarding any policy involving the vehicle or any claim relating to the vehicle;
- The name of any towing service involved in moving or storing the vehicle;

- The name and address of any law enforcement agency to which any incident involving the vehicle was reported;
- The amount of any estimate of damage, loss, or repair costs;
- The name and address of any body shop or repair facility involved;
- The name and address of any other insured owner involved in any such incident; and
- Any and all other information relating to the vehicle.

2.6 Uncovering a Party's Special Culpability

Page 73

2.6.8 Creditor Financing the Sale to the Consumer

Addition to note 258.

258   *Replace NCLC UDAP citation with*: National Consumer Law Center, Unfair and Deceptive Acts and Practices § 10.5.2.4 (8th ed. 2012).

Chapter 3

Automobile Title Law

3.4 Information That Must Be Provided to Transferee on Title Document

3.4.1 Risk of Forgery and Alterations

Page 85

Add to text at end of subsection:

The increased interest among lenders and states to move to electronic titling systems has prompted Congress to enact legislation to enable states to adopt pure electronic titling systems. In 2012, amendments to the Motor Vehicle Information and Cost Savings Act were passed directing the Department of Transportation to prescribe regulations, by January 6, 2014, to allow an electronic disclosure or notice to substitute for any MVICSA-required written disclosure or notice.[61.1] These regulations will likely facilitate the use of electronic titling. While increased usage of electronic titling has the potential to reduce certain forms of titling fraud, it could also introduce other forms of consumer abuse.

> 61.1   *See* Pub. L. No. 112-141, § 31205, 126 Stat. 761 (2012).

3.7 Electronic Liens and Titling

Page 89

Add to text after subsection's second paragraph:

The increased interest in moving to entirely electronic titling systems has prompted Congress to enact legislation enabling states to adopt such systems without having to petition NHTSA for approval of alternative disclosures. In 2012, amendments to the Motor Vehicle Information and Cost Savings Act were passed directing the Department of Transportation to prescribe regulations, by January 6, 2014, to allow an electronic disclosure or notice to substitute for any MVICSA-required written disclosure or notice.[95.1] These regulations will likely facilitate the move to electronic titling. While increased usage of electronic titling has the potential to reduce certain forms of titling fraud, it could also introduce other forms of consumer abuse.

> 95.1   *See* Pub. L. No. 112-141, § 31205, 126 Stat. 761 (2012).

Add to text at end of paragraph containing note 98:

Texas amended its motor vehicle titling laws, consistent with the changes made to permit electronic titling, in 2011.[98.1]

> 98.1   Act of June 17, 2011, 2011 Tex. Sess. Law Serv. 2011 (West) (relating to motor vehicles, amending Texas Transportation, Health and Safety, and Occupational Codes).

3.8 Privacy of Title Information

3.8.2 DPPA Allows DMV to Release Names and Addresses in Selected Circumstances

Page 90

Add to text after subsection's second paragraph:

The permissible purpose of an investigation in anticipation of litigation made as an exception to the prohibition under the DPPA against the release and use of personal information is not limited to investigating the history of individual cars. The permissible purpose may include investigation to show pattern and practice[113.1] or to identify others harmed who may be part of a group or class.[113.2]

> 113.1   *See* Thomas v. George, Hartz, Lundeen, Fulmer, Johnstone, King, & Stevens, P.A., 525 F.3d 1107 (11th Cir. 2008) (even though a number of drivers received "custom and practice" letters, those alleging violation of the DPPA failed to meet their burden of proof when the request was made in response to defendant dealers' claim of a requirement to plead and prove multiple acts of deceptive and unfair acts in order to state a claim).

113.2   *See* Maracich v. Spears, 675 F.3d 281 (4th Cir. 2012) (litigation exception applied to use of information to identify named plaintiffs for a "group action" for the benefit of all others), *cert. granted*, 133 S. Ct. 98 (2012).

Add to text after paragraph containing note 114:

Use of DPPA protected information is permissible "for use by any government agency, including any court or law enforcement agency, in carrying out its functions, or any private person or entity acting on behalf of a Federal, State, or local agency in carrying out its functions." This exception may provide a permissible purpose to private attorneys in consumer cases when acting as private attorneys general.[114.1]

One issue that arises when interpreting the DPPA is the relationship between the various permissible uses. Several circuit courts, including the Eleventh Circuit and the Fourth Circuit, have found that when use is permitted under one of the enumerated permissible uses, it need not comply with requirements found in one of the other enumerated permissible uses.[114.2] Accordingly, if attorneys obtain and use private information for the permissible use of investigation in anticipation of litigation, they need not comply with the requirements of permissible use for solicitation purposes even if they use the information for solicitation.[114.3] However some courts have found that impermissible use is actionable even if the user can point to an additional permissible use that may have been satisfied.[114.4]

114.1   *See* Maracich v. Spears, 675 F.3d 281 (4th Cir. 2012) (dicta discussing use of this exception), *cert. granted*, 133 S. Ct. 98 (2012).

114.2   *See* Rine v. Imagitas, Inc., 590 F.3d 1215 (11th Cir. 2009) (private entity contracted by state to provide renewal information under enumerated state action permissible purpose need not comply with requirements of the solicitation permissible purpose).

114.3   Maracich v. Spears, 675 F.3d 281 (4th Cir. 2012) (use permissible in anticipation of litigation need not comply with requirements of permissible use for solicitation), *cert. granted*, 133 S. Ct. 98 (2012).

114.4   Pichler v. UNITE, 542 F.3d 380 (3d Cir. 2008) (despite some use for litigation purposes, union acquired and used information from department of motor vehicles initially for the impermissible purpose of identifying workers in an attempt to further organizing efforts).

Addition to note 115.

115   *See* Wiles v. Ascom Transp. Sys., Inc., 478 Fed. Appx. 283 (6th Cir. 2012) (bulk purchases by resellers permissible under DPPA); Graczyk v. West Pub. Co., 660 F.3d 275 (7th Cir. 2011); Taylor v. Acxiom Corp., 612 F.3d 325 (5th Cir. 2010).

Replace sentence containing note 116 with:

At least one case has held to the contrary that a service cannot collect information for the purpose of selling it to the general public, even when the service only sells the information to members of the public who have a permissible purpose under the DPPA.[116]

116   Roberts v. The Source for Pub. Data, 2008 WL 52346745 (W.D. Mo. Dec. 12, 2008).

3.9 Remedies for Title Violations

3.9.2 MVICSA Remedies

Page 92

3.9.2.1 Utility of a MVICSA Claim

Replace sentence containing note 131 with:

Violations of federal titling requirements analyzed in this chapter should lead to a private federal cause of action under the Act for treble damages, $10,000 minimum damages,[131] and attorney fees.

131   49 U.S.C. § 32710(a).

The amount of minimum damages was increased by Pub. L. No. 112-141, § 31206, 126 Stat. 761 (2012), effective October 1, 2012. Prior to that date, the statute had specified minimum damages of $1500, although by federal regulation that amount had been increased by an adjustment for inflation. For violations occurring after December 21, 2010, the statutory damages amount had been increased from $2000 to $3000 pursuant to 75 Fed. Reg. 79,978 (Dec. 21, 2010) (amending 49 C.F.R. § 578.6(f)(2)).

Replace note 133 with:

133   *See* National Consumer Law Center, Federal Deception Law Ch. 7 (2012).

Chapter 4	Yo-Yo (Spot-Delivery) Abuses and Sublease Scams

4.1 Getting Started

Page 98

4.1.2 Yo-Yo Transactions Explained

Addition to notes 4, 6.

4   *See In re* Galindo, 467 B.R. 201 (Bankr. S.D. Cal. 2012) (dealer's multiple assurances that the retail installment sales contract had been assigned constituted fraud).

6   *Replace Salvagne v. Fairfield Ford, Inc. citation with*: 794 F. Supp. 2d 826 (S.D. Ohio 2010). *Add to Chastain v. N.S.S. Acquisition Corp. citation: aff'd*, 378 Fed. Appx. 983 (11th Cir. 2010).

Page 99

4.1.4 State Yo-Yo Laws

Replace "Utah" in sentence containing note 7 with:

Texas, Utah

Addition to note 7.

7   Tex. Fin. Code Ann. § 348.013 (West). *See generally* Appx. O, *infra.*

Add to text at end of subsection:

State yo-yo sales statutes are summarized in Appendix O, *infra.*

4.2 Dealer's Right to Cancel the Yo-Yo Transaction

Page 101

4.2.5 Does Contingency Clause Comply with State Law?

Add to text after sentence containing note 26:

Texas law limits the duration of a conditional delivery agreement to fifteen days.[26.1]
26.1   Tex. Fin. Code Ann. § 348.013(e) (West).

Page 102

4.2.7 Have the Exact Conditions Allowing Cancellation Occurred?

Replace note 35 with:

35   *See* National Consumer Law Center, Unfair and Deceptive Acts and Practices § 7.2.4 (8th ed. 2012).

Page 103

4.2.9 Misrepresentations That the Sale Is Final

Addition to note 40.

40   *See In re* Galindo, 467 B.R. 201 (Bankr. S.D. Cal. 2012) (dealer's multiple assurances that the retail installment sales contract had been assigned constituted fraud).

Page 104

Replace note 42 with:

42   *See* National Consumer Law Center, Unfair and Deceptive Acts and Practices §§ 4.2.15, 4.2.19 (8th ed. 2012).

4.2.10 UDAP and Other Consumer Remedies When Cancellation Not Valid

Replace notes 47, 50 with:
Page 105

47   *See* National Consumer Law Center, Unfair and Deceptive Acts and Practices § 2.2.4 (8th ed. 2012).
50   *See* National Consumer Law Center, Unfair and Deceptive Acts and Practices § 2.2.4 (8th ed. 2012).

4.3 Federal Disclosure and Notice Requirements

4.3.1 Introduction

Replace notes 53, 55 with:

53 (8th ed. 2012).

55 National Consumer Law Center, Truth in Lending Ch. 13 (8th ed. 2012).

Addition to note 59.

59 *But see* Nixon v. Enter. Car Sales Co., 2011 WL 4857941 (E.D. Mo. Oct. 13, 2011) (dealer attempting to find finance company to purchase retail installment sales contract in transaction with a spot delivery agreement had a permissible purpose under Fair Credit Reporting Act to pull additional credit reports after first potential assignee refused to buy contract).

Page 106

4.3.2 The Truth in Lending Disclosure Form

Replace sentence containing note 64 with:

The Consumer Financial Protection Bureau's official interpretation of its version of Regulation Z states explicitly that "the consumer receives a copy to keep at the time the consumer becomes obligated," as does the Federal Reserve Board's commentary on its version of the regulation.[64]

64 Consumer Fin. Prot. Bureau, 12 C.F.R. pt. 1026, supp. I, § 1026.17(b) cmt. 3; Fed. Reserve Bd., 12 C.F.R. pt. 226, supp. I, § 226.17(b) cmt. 3.

Addition to note 67.

67 *Replace Hunter v. Bev Smith Ford, L.L.C. appellate citation with*: 353 Fed. Appx. 218 (11th Cir. 2009).

Replace note 69 with:

69 *See* National Consumer Law Center, Truth in Lending § 11.6.5 (8th ed. 2012).

Addition to notes 71, 74.

71 *Replace NCLC Truth in Lending citation with*: National Consumer Law Center, Truth in Lending §§ 4.4.6, 11.5, 11.6.3.4, 11.6.6.2.2 (8th ed. 2012).

Page 107

74 *Replace Salvagne v. Fairfield Ford, Inc. citation with*: 794 F. Supp. 2d 826 (S.D. Ohio 2010). *Add to Chastain v. N.S.S. Acquisition Corp. citation*: *aff'd*, 378 Fed. Appx. 983 (11th Cir. 2010).
    Add: *But see* Vereen v. Lou Sobh Auto. of Jax, Inc., 2012 WL 601217 (M.D. Fla. Feb. 23, 2012) (use of a bailment/spot delivery agreement did not violate TILA even when dealer subsequently demanded buyer agree to less advantageous loan terms and repossessed car when buyer failed to do so).

4.3.3 ECOA and FCRA Notice Requirements

4.3.3.1 General

Addition to notes 77, 78.

77 *Replace first Code of Federal Regulations citation with*: *See* 15 U.S.C. §§ 1691(d), 1691a(e); 12 C.F.R. § 1002.9 [§ 202.9]. *Replace second Code of Federal Regulations citation with*: *But see* 15 U.S.C. § 1691(d)(5) (oral notification sufficient if lender acts on less than 150 applications a year); 12 C.F.R. § 1002.9(d) [§ 202.9(d)].

78 *Replace Code of Federal Regulations citation with*: 12 C.F.R. § 1002.12(b) [§ 202.12(b)].

Page 108

4.3.3.2 Is the Dealer a Covered Creditor Under the ECOA?

Replace sentence containing note 85 with:

Regulation B, which enforces the ECOA, defines creditor as: "[A] person who, in the ordinary course of business, regularly participates in the credit decision, including setting the terms of the credit. The term creditor includes a creditor's assignee, transferee, or subrogee who so participates."[85]

85 12 C.F.R. § 1002.2(*l*) [§ 202.1(*l*)]; *see* 15 U.S.C § 1691a(e).

Replace sentence containing note 87 with:

The ECOA includes arrangers of credit within its definition of creditor,[86.1] and Regulation B further defines arranger of credit as "a person who, in the ordinary course of business, regularly refers applicants or prospective applicants to creditors, or selects or offers to select creditors to whom requests for credit may be made."[87]

86.1 15 U.S.C. § 1691a(e).

87 12 C.F.R. § 1002.2(*l*) [§ 202.1(*l*)].

Replace note 88 with:

88 12 C.F.R. § 1002.2(*l*) [§ 202.1(*l*)]; *see* 15 U.S.C. § 1691a(e) ("The term 'creditor' means . . . any person who regularly arranges for the extension, renewal, or continuation of credit; . . . .").

Page 109

Addition to note 89.

89 *Replace Hunter v. Bev Smith Ford, L.L.C. appellate citation with*: 353 Fed. Appx. 218 (11th Cir. 2009).

4.3.3.3 The Counteroffer Defense

Replace sentence containing note 90 with:

Regulation B requires notice of such a counteroffer within thirty days.[90]

90 12 C.F.R. § 1002.9(a)(1)(i) [§ 202.9(a)(1)(i)]; *see also* National Consumer Law Center, Credit Discrimination Ch. 10 (5th ed. 2009 and Supp.).

Replace note 91 with:

91 15 U.S.C. § 1691(d); 12 C.F.R. §§ 1002.2(c)(1)(ii), 1002.9(a)(1)(iii) [§§ 202.2(c)(1)(ii), 202.9(a)(1)(iii)]; *see also* National Consumer Law Center, Credit Discrimination (5th ed. 2009 and Supp.). *But see* Diaz v. Paragon Motors of Woodside, Inc., 424 F. Supp. 2d 519 (E.D.N.Y. 2006).

4.4 Dealers Almost Always Improperly Structure the Yo-Yo Transaction

Page 110

4.4.1 Dealers Improperly Mix and Match Two Different Types of Transactions

Addition to note 103.

103 *See* Cappo Mgmt. V, Inc. v. Britt, 711 S.E.2d 209 (Va. 2011) (conflict between "Bailment Agreement" provision which stated that car was to remain property of dealer and other contract documents which indicated that ownership transferred at time of sale created ambiguity that must be construed against drafter/dealer).

4.4.3 Dealer Practices Inconsistent with a Condition Precedent Transaction

Page 111

4.4.3.3 TILA Disclosure of Loan Term and APR

Addition to note 109.

109 *Replace NCLC Truth in Lending citation with*: National Consumer Law Center, Truth in Lending § 4.5 (8th ed. 2012). *Replace Salvagne v. Fairfield Ford, Inc. citation with*: 794 F. Supp. 2d 826 (S.D. Ohio 2010). *Add to Chastain v. N.S.S. Acquisition Corp. citation*: aff'd, 378 Fed. Appx. 983 (11th Cir. 2010).

   Add: But see Mack v. Bobbin Trace Auto., L.L.C., 2011 WL 5981017 (N.D. Fla. Nov. 29, 2011) (no TILA violation when cancellation agreement integrated into retail installment sales contract and TILA disclosure documents).

Replace sentence containing note 110 with:

Regulation Z, which enforces TILA, requires the creditor to identify the disclosures as estimates when it does not have information necessary to make accurate disclosures.[110]

110 12 C.F.R. § 1026.17(c)(2) [§ 226.17(c)(2)].

Page 112

Addition to note 111.

111 *Replace NCLC Truth in Lending citation with*: National Consumer Law Center, Truth in Lending § 5.5.6.2 (8th ed. 2012).

4.4.3.5 Excess Insurance Premiums and Related Finance Charges

Addition to note 113.

113 *Replace NCLC Truth in Lending citation with*: National Consumer Law Center, Truth in Lending § 3.9.4.7 (8th ed. 2012).

4.4.4 Dealer Practices Inconsistent with a Condition Subsequent Transaction

Page 113

4.4.4.1 Titling Practices

Replace note 119 with:

119 *See* National Consumer Law Center, Unfair and Deceptive Acts and Practices § 7.4.3 (8th ed. 2012).

Page 115

4.4.4.3 Condition Subsequent Sales Must Comply with UCC Article 9

Addition to notes 133, 136.

133 *See* Cappo Mgmt. V, Inc. v. Britt, 711 S.E.2d 209 (Va. 2011) (dealer must comply with U.C.C. Article 9, including notice of disposition, when attempting to retake vehicle pursuant to condition subsequent provision).
136 *See In re* Galindo, 467 B.R. 201 (Bankr. S.D. Cal. 2012) (dealer's repossession unjustified when dealer helped consumer set up allotment payment to alleged assignee but demanded payments already paid alleged assignee after assignee refused to purchase the loan).

4.5 Illegal Practices Accompanying a Cancellation

4.5.1 Refusing to Return Trade-Ins and Deposits

Page 116

Add to text at end of subsection's second paragraph:

Texas requires return of the trade-in vehicle or, if it cannot be returned, the refund of its agreed value as stated on the conditional delivery agreement.[146.1]

   146.1   Tex. Fin. Code Ann. § 348.013 (West).

Page 118

Add to text after sentence containing note 162:

In Louisiana a dealer retaining a consumer's trade-in after reporting the newly purchased car as stolen and retaking it was found to have committed conversion.[162.1]

   162.1   McFadden v. Import One, Inc., 56 So. 3d 1212 (La. Ct. App. 2011).

Add to text before subsection's last paragraph:

For a variety of reasons some dealers may try to structure the transaction as one in which the consumer or a family member allegedly sells the trade-in to the dealer in a separate transaction and the dealer then treats the sale proceeds as a cash down payment, even though no cash actually changes hands.[169.1] This practice may be an attempt to defraud the potential assignee or conceivably to avoid having to return the trade-in in the event the sale is canceled. In either case the courts should look to the substance of the transaction to determine the rights of the parties.

   169.1   *See In re* Galindo, 467 B.R. 201 (Bankr. S.D. Cal. 2012) (dealer allegedly bought consumer's wife's car in separate sale and claimed proceeds used as cash down payment on purchased car, although no proceeds from the sale were in fact ever paid to consumer or his wife).

4.5.2 Malicious Prosecution When Consumer Does Not Return the Vehicle

Page 119

Addition to note 177.

   177   *See also* McFadden v. Import One, Inc., 56 So. 3d 1212 (La. Ct. App. 2011) ($1000 award for embarrassment and humiliation for having car taken at consumer's place of work by police was not abusively high and in fact amount may be abusively low, although the consumer did not raise this issue on appeal).

4.6 Misrepresentations Involving a Second Transaction

4.6.1 Renegotiation Misrepresentations

Replace note 184 with:

   184   *See* Ohio Admin. Code 109:4-3-16(B)(17); *see also* National Consumer Law Center, Unfair and Deceptive Acts and Practices § 7.5.2 (8th ed. 2012).

4.6.2 Backdating Documentation of a Subsequent Sale

Page 120

Replace notes 188, 189 with:

   188   12 C.F.R. § 1026 app. J(b) [§ 226 app. J(b)].
   189   12 C.F.R. § 1026.2(a)(13) [§ 226.2(a)(13)].

4.7 Yo-Yo Litigation

4.7.1 Must the Consumer Arbitrate Yo-Yo Sale Claims?

Replace note 191 with:

   191   National Consumer Law Center, Consumer Arbitration Agreements (6th ed. 2011 and Supp.); National Consumer Law Center, Unfair and Deceptive Acts and Practices § 11.5.8 (8th ed. 2012).

Addition to note 192.

   192   *But see* Wickersham v. Lynch Motor Co. of Auburn, Inc., 2012 WL 715322 (M.D. Ala. Mar. 6, 2012) (granting dealer's motion to compel arbitration in yo-yo case when consumer failed to respond to motion).

4.7.2 Discovery in Yo-Yo Sale Cases

Page 121

Add to text after seventh bulleted item in subsection:

• Any video or audio recording of any portion of the sale and financing transaction. An increasing number of dealership are video recording customer transactions in the dealer's finance office. Estimates are that ten percent or more of dealerships record these transactions.[195.1]

195.1   *See* Amy Wilson, *Pros and Cons of Videotaping F & I Deals*, Auto. News, June 6, 2012.

Page 122

4.7.3 Consumer Recoveries

Addition to note 197.

197   *See also* Givens v. Van Devere, Inc., 2012 WL 4092803 (N.D. Ohio Apr. 27, 2012) (discussing issue of actual damages in relation to class certification).

4.8 Automobile Subleases

Page 123

4.8.2 Consumer Remedies

Replace note 201 with:

201   15 U.S.C. § 1667(3); 12 C.F.R. § 1013.2(h) [§ 213.2(h)].

Delete note 202.

202   [*Reserved.*]

Replace note 205 with:

205   National Consumer Law Center, Truth in Lending Ch. 13 (8th ed. 2012).

Chapter 5

Federal and State Odometer Requirements

5.2 Scope of the Federal Act

Page 128

5.2.3 *What Is an Odometer?*

Add to text at end of subsection's first paragraph:

The Act's definition of an odometer has now been amended to include not only an "instrument" but also a "system of components."[32.1]

32.1 Pub. L. No. 112-141, § 31205, 126 Stat. 760 (2012) (effective October 1, 2012).

Add to text at end of subsection:

In modern vehicles the starting point for odometer data is the vehicle speed sensor (VSS). The sensor sends a stream of either analog or digital pulses per revolution of the driveshaft or final drive gear. Some vehicles also use a wheel speed sensor. A large number of vehicles store the data in the dash or cluster module. Others store it in the engine control module or in both the dash and the engine control modules. Retrieval of information stored in digital format goes through the data display module.

5.3 Restrictions on Odometer Tampering

Page 130

5.3.3 *Selling of Unlawful Odometer Devices*

Replace note 62 with:

62 *See* Baxter v. Kawasaki Motors Corp., __ F. Supp. 2d __, 2012 WL 5877530 (N.D. Ill. Nov. 13, 2012).

Add to text after sentence containing note 62:

Nor do courts in such a situation typically find facts showing an intent to defraud, which is required to recover under the Act.[62.1] One court, in interpreting state law, found that an odometer is legal if it meets the state's approved tolerance of accuracy of being within four percent of actual mileage, unless the designer or manufacturer deliberately miscalibrated the odometer.[62.2]

62.1 *See* Baxter v. Kawasaki Motors Corp., __ F. Supp. 2d __, 2012 WL 5877530 (N.D. Ill. Nov. 13, 2012).
62.2 *See* Lopez v. Nissan N. Am., Inc., 135 Cal. Rptr. 3d 116 (Ct. App. 2012).

5.6 Disclosure Requirements

5.6.3 *Transfers for Which Disclosures Must Be Made*

Page 134

5.6.3.2 Repossessions, Transfers to Insurers, and Other Involuntary Transfers

Replace note 105 with:

105 Roach v. Middleton Auto Sales, Inc., 623 F. Supp. 2d 139 (D. Mass. 2009), *aff'd sub nom.* Roach v. CUNA Mut. Ins. Co., 385 Fed. Appx. 2 (1st Cir. 2010).

5.6.5 *Method of Making Disclosures*

Page 140

5.6.5.4 Use of Separate Disclosure in Transfer of Used Vehicle

Replace note 159 with:

159 *See* § 9.4.5, *infra*; National Consumer Law Center, Unfair and Deceptive Acts and Practices § 4.2.15 (8th ed. 2012).

Page 144

5.6.5.7 Alternative State Disclosure Systems for Electronic Titles

Add to text at end of subsection:

In July 2012 Congress enacted a requirement that the Department of Transportation prescribe regulations by January 6, 2014 which would allow an electronic disclosure or notice to substitute for any written disclosure or notice required by the Federal Act.[208.1] This change should facilitate the move in many states to electronic titling, which has the potential both to reduce certain forms of titling fraud and also to introduce other forms of consumer abuse.

208.1   Pub. L. No. 112-141, § 31205, 126 Stat. 761 (2012).

5.6.7 Non-Mileage Disclosures

Page 151

5.6.7.1 Content of Non-Mileage Disclosures

Add note 272.1 after "year" in subsection's fourth bulleted point.

272.1   A vehicle's year designation can be complicated in the case of multi-stage vehicles—when one manufacturer produces a body, but another manufacturer completes the vehicle. A good discussion of this issue is found in Anderson v. Gulf Stream Coach, Inc., 662 F.3d 775 (7th Cir. 2011).

5.8 The Intent Requirement

Page 154

5.8.3 General Standards Concerning Proof of Intent

Addition to note 330.

330   *Add to Enobakhare v. Carpoint, L.L.C. citation*: (mag.), *adopted by* 2011 WL 704902 (E.D.N.Y. Feb. 16, 2011).

Chapter 6	# Remedies for MVICSA and State Odometer Act Violations

6.2 Standing in Private Actions; No Privity Required

Page 164

6.2.3 Plaintiff Need Not Be Current Title Owner

Addition to note 14.

14   *See also* Davco Constr. Co. v. Dom Italiano's Used Car Corner, Inc., 1997 WL 433595 (Ohio Ct. App. July 24, 1997) (plaintiff can pursue action under state odometer statute even if plaintiff no longer owns vehicle at time of filing complaint).

6.4 Statute of Limitations

Page 167

6.4.2 Statute of Limitations Under State Odometer Acts

Replace note 39 with:

39   *See* National Consumer Law Center, Unfair and Deceptive Acts and Practices § 11.2 (8th ed. 2012).

6.4.3 Use of Counterclaim or Recoupment When Statute of Limitations Has Run

Addition to note 40.

40   *Replace NCLC Truth in Lending citation with*: National Consumer Law Center, Truth in Lending § 12.2.5 (8th ed. 2012). *Replace NCLC UDAP citation with*: National Consumer Law Center, Unfair and Deceptive Acts and Practices § 11.2.5 (8th ed. 2012).

Replace note 41 with:

41   *See* § 10.4.4, *infra*; *see also* National Consumer Law Center, Unfair and Deceptive Acts and Practices § 10.5 (8th ed. 2012).

6.6 Choosing Between State and Federal Claims and Courts

Page 168

6.6.1 Claim Selection Largely Determines Court Selection

Replace note 51 with:

51   *See* § 10.4.4, *infra. See generally* National Consumer Law Center, Unfair and Deceptive Acts and Practices § 10.5 (8th ed. 2012).

Addition to note 52.

52   *Replace NCLC UDAP citation with*: National Consumer Law Center, Federal Deception Law § 4.3.4.3 (2012); National Consumer Law Center, Unfair and Deceptive Acts and Practices § 10.5.2.4 (8th ed. 2012).

Page 169

6.6.3 Benefits of Adding a State Odometer Claim to a Federal Act Claim

Replace note 60 with:

60   *See* National Consumer Law Center, Unfair and Deceptive Acts and Practices § 11.2 (8th ed. 2012).

6.8 Private Remedies

6.8.1 Treble Damages

6.8.1.1 General

Page 170

In subsection's first paragraph replace "$3000" each time it occurs with:

$10,000

Addition to note 74.

74   *Add at end of note*: Effective October 1, 2012, minimum damages have increased to $10,000. *See* § 6.8.2.1 (Supp.), *infra*.

Page 171

Add to text at end of subsection's third paragraph:

An Ohio appellate court has decided that the consumer can recover both actual damages under one state law claim and treble those damages under the Ohio odometer statute because the Ohio statute provides that remedies under the state odometer statute are in addition to those available under other causes of action.[79.1] Recovery was allowed even though other parties had settled the case and thus the plaintiff had already recovered some of the actual damages that were trebled.[79.2]

79.1   Davco Constr. Co. v. Dom Italiano's Used Car Corner, Inc., 1997 WL 433595 (Ohio Ct. App. July 24, 1997).
79.2   *Id.*

6.8.2 Minimum Statutory Damages Awards Under the Federal Act

Page 175

Replace § 6.8.2.1 heading with:

6.8.2.1 Minimum Damages Are $10,000 Effective October 1, 2012

Replace subsection's first sentence with:

The Federal Act now specifies that a person violating the Act with an intent to defraud is liable for private remedies of the greater of treble damages or $10,000. This increase in amount to $10,000 was enacted July 6, 2012, and became effective on October 1, 2012.[114.1]

Prior to that, the statute specified that defendants were liable for the greater of treble damages or $1500. But even this number had been increased.

114.1   Pub. L. No. 112-141, § 31206, 126 Stat. 761 (2012).

Page 178

6.8.4 Attorney Fees

Addition to note 151.

151   *Replace NCLC Truth in Lending citation with*: National Consumer Law Center, Truth in Lending § 11.9 (8th ed. 2012).

Page 179

6.8.5 Costs

Replace note 159 with:

159   *See* National Consumer Law Center, Truth in Lending § 11.9.4.5 (8th ed. 2012).

6.9 Government Enforcement

6.9.1 Federal Enforcement

Page 180

6.9.1.2 Civil Penalties Sought by the United States Department of Transportation

Replace subsection's first sentence with:

Effective October 1, 2012, a person who violates the Federal Act, its regulations, or an order issued under the statute may be liable to the federal government for a civil penalty not to exceed $10,000 for each separate violation.[172.1] Prior to that date the penalty was $3200.[173]

172.1   Pub. L. No. 112-141, § 31206, 126 Stat. 761 (2012).
173   *[Retain as in main volume.]*

Replace sentence containing note 174 with:

Effective October 1, 2012, the maximum penalty for a related series of violations is $1 million.[173.1] Prior to that date the maximum penalty was $140,000.[174]

173.1   Pub. L. No. 112-141, § 31206, 126 Stat. 761 (2012).
174   *[Retain as in main volume.]*

Chapter 7

Other Statutes Specifically Relating to Automobile Fraud

7.2 Statutes Dealing with Disclosure of Vehicle's Prior Physical Damage

7.2.1 State Salvage Vehicle Statutes

Page 184

7.2.1.3 Persons Covered

Add note 16.1 at end of subsection's first sentence.

16.1 *See* Storie v. Randy's Auto Sales, L.L.C., 589 F.3d 873 (7th Cir. 2009) (Indiana salvage title law applies to "any person," including dealers, not just insurance companies).

Add to text at end of subsection:

Sometimes an entity that acquires a salvage vehicle may have already resold the vehicle before it gets possession of the certificate of title. For example, in one case an insurance company acquired a total loss vehicle. It applied for a certificate of title, but did not apply for a salvage title. Before the title was issued, it sold the vehicle to an Indiana car dealer, which then resold the vehicle nine days later—still before the certificate of title was issued. When the title was finally issued, the insurer forwarded the title to the dealer, which forwarded it in turn to the buyer.[18.1] The Indiana Supreme Court held that the dealer had an obligation to apply for a salvage title even though the dealer no longer owned the vehicle when it finally got possession of the certificate of title.[18.2]

18.1 *See* Storie v. Randy's Auto Sales, L.L.C., 589 F.3d 873 (7th Cir. 2009) (reciting these facts).
18.2 Storie v. Randy's Auto Sales, L.L.C., 926 N.E.2d 487 (Ind. 2010).

Page 186

7.2.1.6 Titling, Resale, and Disclosure

Addition to note 37.

37 *CALIFORNIA: See also* Cal. Code Regs. tit. 13, § 260.03 (statements of vehicle condition must accurately reflect the known condition).
 COLORADO: Replace statutory citation with: Colo. Rev. Stat. § 6-1-708(1)(b).
 IDAHO: Replace statutory citation with: Idaho Code Ann. § 49-524(8).
 INDIANA: Ind. Code § 9-22-3-18.5 (identical to § 9-22-3-30 except that it includes an express exception for golf carts).
 MAINE: Replace Maine Code of Regulations citation with: 29-250-104 Me. Code R. § 1(F) (LexisNexis).
 MINNESOTA: Replace "seventy" in explanatory parenthetical following Minn. Stat. § 325F.6641 with: eighty.
 Add new entry: TEXAS: Tex. Transp. Code Ann. § 501.109 (West) (unlawful to make knowing sale, transfer, or release of a salvage motor vehicle in violation of Certificate of Title Act, which makes it an offense for a person to apply for a title for a vehicle if that person knows or reasonably should know that the vehicle is a nonrepairable vehicle that has been repaired, rebuilt, or reconstructed).

Page 189

7.2.1.9 Interstate Transfers of Salvage Vehicles

Addition to note 58.

58 *See, e.g.,* Storie v. Randy's Auto Sales, L.L.C., 589 F.3d 873 (7th Cir. 2009) (concluding that transferee state's title law applies, not transferor state's title law).

Add to text at end of subsection:

Another question is which state's salvage vehicle statute applies when a vehicle is transferred from one state to another. In an Indiana case an insurance company acquired a total loss vehicle. It applied for a Tennessee certificate of title, but did not apply for a salvage title. Before the title was issued, it sold the vehicle to an Indiana car dealer. The Seventh Circuit held that Indiana's titling law, not Tennessee's, applied to the Indiana dealer.[61.1]

61.1 Storie v. Randy's Auto Sales, L.L.C., 589 F.3d 873 (7th Cir. 2009).

7.2.1.10 Remedies

Addition to notes 63, 64, 71, 75, 77.

63   Pedroza v. Lomas Auto Mall, Inc., 600 F. Supp. 2d 1200 (D.N.M. 2009) (knowingly seeking clean title for vehicle when state law requires salvage title is UDAP violation).

64   Ind. Code §§ 9-22-3-36 (allowing person aggrieved by violation of salvage title laws to sue for actual damages and attorney fees; court has discretion to treble damages or award $2500, whichever is greater), 9-22-3-37 (violation of salvage title laws is UDAP violation); *see* Storie v. Randy's Auto Sales, L.L.C., 2011 WL 2470598 (S.D. Ind. June 17, 2011) (questioning whether buyer was aggrieved when he would not have seen salvage title until after sale even if dealer had obtained one).

Page 190

71   *Delete Storie v. Randy's Auto Sales, L.L.C. citation.*
        Add: But see Storie v. Randy's Auto Sales, L.L.C., 2011 WL 2470598 (S.D. Ind. June 17, 2011) (denying fraud claim; dealership lacked fraudulent intent when it reasonably believed, based on ambiguous state law, that it did not have duty to obtain salvage title).

75   *But see* Martinez v. Ford Motor Credit Co., 2012 WL 3711347 (Tex. App. Aug. 29, 2012) (unpublished) (taking extremely narrow view of negligence per se; claim unavailable because stated purposes of certificate of title law, of which salvage titling law is a part, are theft prevention and disclosure of liens, not vehicle safety or prevention of fraud, so consumer does not belong to class law was intended to protect).

77   *Replace Idaho statutory citation with*: Idaho Code Ann. § 49-524(8). *Add parenthetical to Washington statutory citation*: (class C felony for a person to remove the marking indicating that the vehicle was previously destroyed or declared a total loss).

7.2.2 Used Car Damage Disclosure Statutes

7.2.2.1 Overview

Addition to note 80.

80   *Replace Colorado statutory citation with*: Colo. Rev. Stat. § 6-1-708(1)(b).

Page 191

7.2.2.2 Requirements and Interpretations

Replace "verify" in Alaska paragraph's first sentence with:

sign

Replace note 84 with:

84   Colo. Rev. Stat. § 6-1-708(1)(b).

Page 192

Replace note 100 with:

100   *See* National Consumer Law Center, Unfair and Deceptive Acts and Practices § 4.2.19.3 (8th ed. 2012).

Page 194

Addition to note 136.

136   *See also* Martin v. Extreme Auto Sales Plus, Inc., 809 N.W.2d 901 (Wis. Ct. App. 2012) (table) (dealer could not assert "as is/warranty disclaimer" provision of contract as a defense to plaintiff's claim for repairs even though it revealed all vehicle defects in Buyers Guide, when vehicle could not be legally operated at time of sale but contract did not include warning required by regulation).

7.2.3 New Car Damage Disclosure Statutes

7.2.3.2 Threshold Amounts of Damage Requiring Disclosure

Page 195

Addition to note 144.

144   *Cf.* Bourgi v. W. Covina Motors, Inc., 2011 WL 2207477 (Cal. Ct. App. June 8, 2011) (unpublished) (dealer may make repairs by replacing damaged parts with non-original manufacturer parts; even if repairs are imperfect, damage need not be disclosed as long as cost does not bring total repair cost over three percent threshold).

Page 197

7.2.3.6 Remedies

Addition to note 166.

166   *Replace NCLC UDAP citation with*: National Consumer Law Center, Unfair and Deceptive Acts and Practices § 3.2.7 (8th ed. 2012).

7.2.3.7 Statutes Shield Dealers from Consumer Remedies When Threshold Damage Amount Is Not Reached

Replace note 173 with:

173   *See* § 9.4, *infra*; National Consumer Law Center, Unfair and Deceptive Acts and Practices § 7.5.4 (8th ed. 2012).

Add to text after sentence containing note 173:	In addition, the statute may allow the dealer not to disclose only a certain type of damage, such as pre-delivery damage, leaving unaffected any duty under other law to disclose damage that occurs on the dealer's lot.[173.1]

    173.1   *See, e.g.*, Smith v. Casey Chevrolet Corp., 68 Va. Cir. 238 (2005).

Page 198	### 7.2.5 Dealer Responsibility to Inspect Vehicles

Addition to notes 180, 182.	180 Conn. Gen. Stat. § 14-62(g) ("Before offering any used motor vehicle for retail sale, the selling dealer shall complete a comprehensive safety inspection of such vehicle.").
	182 *See* Garcia Auto Sales, Inc. v. Strachan, 2012 WL 4294127 (R.I. Super. Ct. Sept. 17, 2012) (affirming motor vehicle dealer licensing board's order that dealer repurchase vehicle that it illegally sold without an inspection sticker, and reimburse buyer for costs to repair car to pass inspection; "[H]ad the Dealership simply followed the law and had the Vehicle inspected—which it should have known to do given that it has been in business for many years—the repairs to the Vehicle would have been unnecessary.").

Page 199	## 7.3 Statutes Dealing with Disclosure of Vehicle's Prior Use

Addition to notes 206, 208.	206 *Replace explanatory parenthetical to Cal. Code Regs. tit. 13, § 260.02 citation with*: (express advertisements (broadly defined to include any statement to any member of the public) of vehicle's prior use or ownership history must be accurate; former taxicabs, rental vehicles, publicly owned vehicles, insurance salvage vehicles and revived salvage vehicles shall be clearly identified as such if previous status is known to seller; dealer must disclose if "demonstrator" was previously registered or sold to a retail purchaser). *Replace "37 Pa. Code § 301.4(2)(iii)" with*: 37 Pa. Code § 301.4(a)(2)(iii).

        Add: Olah v. Ganley Chevrolet, Inc., 946 N.E.2d 771 (Ohio Ct. App. 2010) (evidence did not support finding that dealer had knowledge vehicle was a "factory official vehicle" that would give rise to a duty to disclose prior use; although vehicle was purchased at auction and auction slip showed that vehicle was previously owned by manufacturer and used as a company vehicle, there was nothing to show the extent of the vehicle's use).

    208   *See* Whited v. Galindo (*In re* Galindo), 467 B.R. 201, 209 (Bankr. S.D. Cal. 2012) (violation of department of motor vehicles regulation requiring disclosure of prior use is violation of California Consumers Legal Remedies Act).

Add to text at end of sentence containing note 208:	or fraud.[208.1]

    208.1   *See In re* Galindo, 467 B.R. 201, 209 (Bankr. S.D. Cal. 2012) (dealership employee's false statements regarding prior use of former rental car amounted to fraud in light of department of motor vehicles regulation requiring disclosure of prior rental history if known to dealer).

Addition to notes 212, 213. *Page 200*	212 *Replace Montana Administrative Code citation with*: Mont. Admin. R. 23.19.204. 213 Cal. Code Regs. tit. 13, § 255.02 ("demonstrator").

7.5 State Airbag Laws

Addition to notes 221, 224, 227. *Page 201*	221 *Replace Florida statutory citation with*: Fla. Stat. §§ 860.145, 860.146. *Add: See also* P.R. Laws Ann. tit. 9, § 2078.
	224 *See also* Cal. Admin. Code tit. 16, § 3367 (automobile repair dealer shall not install, distribute, or sell air bag that is known or should be known to have been previously deployed).
	227 *Replace Utah statutory citation with*: Utah Code Ann. § 41-6a-1624 (West).

7.6 State Lemon Laundering Statutes

7.6.1 General

Replace note 229 with:	229 *See, e.g.*, Harmon v. Major Chrysler Jeep Dodge, Inc., 955 N.Y.S.2d 357 (App. Div. 2012) (seller violated lemon laundering statute when disclosure that car was a returned lemon was dated after signature of purchase contract). *See generally* Appx. C, *infra*.

Page 203	### 7.6.4 Lack of Privity Should Not Be a Defense to a Lemon Laundering Claim

Replace note 237 with:	237 *See* National Consumer Law Center, Unfair and Deceptive Acts and Practices § 4.2.19 (8th ed. 2012).

7.7 Dealer Licensing Statutes

Page 205

7.7.4 *Compliance with State Title Laws*

Addition to note 266.

266   *Replace "625 Ill. Comp. Stat. § 5/5-501(2)" with*: 625 Ill. Comp. Stat. § 5/5-501(a)(2).

Page 206

7.7.5 *Performance of Sales Contracts, Violations of Odometer Laws, and Fraud*

Addition to notes 267, 269.

267   *Delete South Dakota statutory citation's explanatory parenthetical.*

269   *Replace Iowa statutory citation with*: Iowa Code § 322.6(1)(i).

Page 208

7.9 Special Statutory Causes of Action for Automobile Fraud

Replace notes 291, 295 with:
Page 209

291   *See* National Consumer Law Center, Unfair and Deceptive Acts and Practices § 11.4.3.2 (8th ed. 2012).

295   *See* National Consumer Law Center, Unfair and Deceptive Acts and Practices § 11.4.3.3 (8th ed. 2012).

Addition to note 314.

314   *Replace Two Old Hippies, L.L.C. v. Catch the Bus, L.L.C. citation with*: 784 F. Supp. 2d 1200 (D.N.M. 2011).

Page 210

Replace note 320 with:

320   *See* National Consumer Law Center, Unfair and Deceptive Acts and Practices § 11.4.3.6 (8th ed. 2012).

Addition to note 329.

329   *Replace NCLC UDAP citation with*: National Consumer Law Center, Unfair and Deceptive Acts and Practices § 2.3.3.3.2 (8th ed. 2012).

Page 211

Replace note 338 with:

338   *See* National Consumer Law Center, Unfair and Deceptive Acts and Practices § 11.4.3.7 (8th ed. 2012).

Chapter 8

Common Law Fraud, Deceit, and Misrepresentation

Page 213

8.1 Advantages and Disadvantages

Addition to note 11.

11 *Replace NCLC UDAP citation with*: National Consumer Law Center, Federal Deception Law § 7.7.2 (2012) (discussion of Rule 9(b) pleading requirements in the context of RICO actions).

8.3 Material Misrepresentations

8.3.3 Fraud by Affirmative Statements

Page 216

8.3.3.2 Fact Versus Opinion

Addition to notes 35, 41, 42.
Page 217

35 *Replace Italian Cowboy Partners, Ltd. v. Prudential Ins. Co. citation with*: 341 S.W.3d 323 (Tex. 2011).

41 *Replace Glenn Constr. Co. v. Bell Aerospace Services, Inc. citation with*: 785 F. Supp. 2d 1258 (M.D. Ala. 2011).
 Add: But cf. Walker v. Harrison, 75 Va. Cir. 319 (2008) (dealer's statement that car would run beautifully and would have no problems, and that he would fix any problems and refund purchase price, relate to future events and cannot be basis of fraud claim).

42 *Replace Robinson v. Sovran Acquisition Ltd. P'ship citation with*: 70 So. 3d 390 (Ala. Civ. App. 2011).

8.3.5 Fraud by Silence (Nondisclosure)

Page 221

8.3.5.3 Seller's Superior Knowledge

Addition to note 80.

80 *See, e.g.*, Bodiford v. Atlanta Fine Cars, Inc., 2012 WL 5428358 (N.D. Ga. Nov. 7, 2012) (denying dealer's motion for summary judgment; withholding information that vehicle was rebuilt may be fraud).

Page 225

8.3.6 Automobile Fraud Precedent Listed by Type of Misrepresentation

Addition to note 107.

107 *But cf.* Crawford v. Stan, 2012 WL 3259760 (Ohio Ct. App. Aug. 6, 2012) (unpublished) (dismissing fraud claim; private seller had no duty to disclose that previous owner had returned car as lemon, and statement that vehicle had no problems was not fraudulent when previous defects had been repaired before seller bought car and it did not have significant problems while he owned it).

8.4 *Scienter*—the Seller's Knowledge That the Representation Is Misleading

Page 230

8.4.2 Whose Knowledge?

Addition to note 123.

123 Whited v. Galindo (*In re* Galindo), 467 B.R. 201, 208–209 (Bankr. S.D. Cal. 2012) (dealership's owner, who was holder of department of motor vehicles license and who knew of vehicle's rental history, is liable for salesperson's misrepresentation and nondisclosure).

8.4.3 Degree of Knowledge

Page 232

8.4.3.2 Actual Knowledge

Addition to note 143.

143 Kesling v. Hubler Nissan, Inc., 975 N.E.2d 367 (Ind. Ct. App. 2012).

Page 233

8.4.3.3 Recklessness

Addition to note 147.

147   *See also* Dumbri v. Convest, Inc., 2010 WL 4064081 (Pa. C.P. Apr. 19, 2010) (dealer may be liable for fraud if it should have known of frame damage). *But cf.* Paulk v. Thomasville Ford Lincoln Mercury, Inc., 732 S.E.2d 297 (Ga. Ct. App. 2012) (salesperson's statement that he was not sure about vehicle's history was not fraud when Carfax report did not show accident, even though consumer's expert testified that damage would be obvious to anyone in used car business).

Page 236

8.4.3.5 Negligent Misrepresentation

Addition to notes 177, 180.

177   Revellini v. Staron, 2012 WL 6634769 (Conn. Super. Ct. Nov. 30, 2012) (awarding damages on negligent misrepresentation claim when seller knew or should have known of vehicle's collision history).

Page 237

180   *See, e.g.,* Branin v. TMC Enterprises, L.L.C., 832 F. Supp. 2d 646 (W.D. Va. 2011) (economic loss rule bars claim of innocent or negligent misrepresentation that odometer reading was accurate); Dumbri v. Convest, Inc., 2010 WL 4064081 (Pa. C.P. Apr. 19, 2010) (economic loss rule bars claim that dealer negligently misrepresented that car had not suffered damage).

8.5 Intent to Induce

8.5.1 General

Page 238

Addition to note 192.

192   *But cf.* Storie v. Randy's Auto Sales, L.L.C., 2011 WL 2470598 (S.D. Ind. June 17, 2011) (no fraud liability when dealer believed salvage title was not required, as he had no intent to deceive).

8.5.2 Remote Sellers and Others Not in Privity with Buyer

Addition to note 194.

194   *Replace Branin v. TMC Enterprises, L.L.C. citation with*: 832 F. Supp. 2d 646 (W.D. Va. 2011).

8.6 Justifiable Reliance

8.6.2 Proving Reliance

Page 241

Addition to note 222.

222   *See also* Whited v. Galindo (*In re* Galindo), 467 B.R. 201, 209 (Bankr. S.D. Cal. 2012) (proof of reliance unnecessary when party with duty to disclose material fact fails to do so).

8.6.3 When Is Reliance Justifiable?

Page 243

Addition to notes 235, 241.

235   *See, e.g.,* Isbell v. Credit Nation Lending Serv., L.L.C., 735 S.E.2d 46 (Ga. Ct. App. 2012) (denying fraud claim on ground that consumers did not exercise due diligence when they proceeded with purchase without waiting for seller to respond to request for vehicle history report, and did not have car inspected even though they were warned it might have a bent frame).

Page 244

241   *Replace Mike Brooks Car World, Inc. v. Sudduth citation with*: 54 So. 3d 364 (Ala. Civ. App. 2010).

8.7 Proof of the Fraud Claim

8.7.2 Parol Evidence Rule

Page 246

Addition to note 264.

264   *But see* Olah v. Ganley Chevrolet, Inc., 946 N.E.2d 771 (Ohio Ct. App. 2010) (parol evidence rule bars claim that seller committed fraud and UDAP violation by representing vehicle as new, when contract stated it was used).

8.8 Defenses

8.8.2 Effect of "As Is" Clause

Page 248

Addition to note 273.

273   *But see* Roberts v. Lanigan Auto Sales, __ S.W.3d __, 2013 WL 44020 (Ky. Ct. App. Jan. 4, 2013).

8.10 Punitive or Exemplary Damages

Page 257

8.10.2 Actual Damages As Precondition to Punitive Damages

Addition to note 352.

352 Abner v. Kan. City S. R.R. Co., 513 F.3d 154 (5th Cir. 2008) (punitive damages can be awarded in Title VII case even when no compensatory damages are awarded; upholding $125,000 punitive damages award when jury found liability but no damages and judge awarded $1 nominal damages).

8.10.3 Are Punitive Damages Available When the Plaintiff Seeks Rescission?

Addition to note 355.

355 *See, e.g.*, Epsman v. Martin-Landers, L.L.C., 64 U.C.C. Rep. Serv. 2d 19 (E.D. Ark. 2007) (buyer who rescinds or revokes acceptance may still recover punitive damages for fraud).

Page 261

8.10.5 Liability of Principals for Punitive Damages Due to the Conduct of Their Agents

Addition to note 388.

388 *See* Lawlor v. N. Am. Corp. of Ill., __ N.E.2d __, 2012 WL 4950860, at *12 (Ill. Oct. 18, 2012) (punitive damages proper if principal authorized agent's act); Mattyasovszky v. W. Towns Bus Co., 330 N.E.2d 509, 512 (Ill. 1975).

Page 262

8.10.6 State Statute May Limit Size of Punitive Damages Award

Add to text at end of Arkansas paragraph:

However, in 2011 the Arkansas Supreme Court struck down this latter statute as a violation of the provision of the state constitution which prohibits laws limiting the amount to be recovered for death or for injuries to persons or to property.[396.1]

396.1 Bayer CropScience Ltd. P'ship v. Schafer, __ S.W.3d __, 2011 WL 6091323 (Ark. Dec. 8, 2011).

Add to text at end of Connecticut paragraph:

In addition, there is a long-standing common-law doctrine in Connecticut that measures punitive damages by litigation costs, as a way of making the plaintiff whole.[399.1]

399.1 Berry v. Loiseau, 614 A.2d 414, 434 (Conn. 1992).

Page 263

Replace note 412 with:

412 Jones v. United Parcel Serv., Inc., 658 F. Supp. 2d 1308 (D. Kan. 2009), *aff'd in relevant part*, 674 F.3d 1187 (10th Cir. 2012).

Replace final sentence of Missouri paragraph with:

They also are inapplicable to civil actions alleging discrimination. The Missouri Supreme Court upheld the statute against a variety of challenges in 2012.[414.1]

414.1 Estate of Overbey v. Chad Franklin Nat'l Auto Sales N., L.L.C., 361 S.W.3d 364 (Mo. 2012).

Page 264

Replace sentence containing note 424 with:

The state supreme court also reversed several intermediate appellate court decisions holding that the statute's requirement that the punitive damages determination be bifurcated from the compensatory damages determination violates the state constitution, on the ground that the state constitution gave the state supreme court exclusive authority to prescribe rules of court. The supreme court held that the statute created a *substantive* right to bifurcation in tort actions including claims for both compensatory and punitive damages.[424]

424 Havel v. Villa St. Joseph, 963 N.E.2d 1270 (Ohio 2012); *see also* Myers v. Brown, 950 N.E.2d 213 (Ohio Ct. App. 2011), *rev'd*, 967 N.E.2d 1212 (Ohio 2012); Plaugher v. Oniala, 2011 WL 883984 (Ohio Ct. App. Mar. 14, 2011), *rev'd*, 967 N.E.2d 1213 (Ohio 2012).

Replace first sentence of Oregon paragraph with:

Or. Rev. Stat. § 31.735 provides that thirty percent of any punitive damages award will go to the prevailing party, sixty percent to the attorney general for the Department of Justice Crime Victims' Assistance Section, and ten percent to the attorney general for the State Court Facilities and Security account.

Replace "this statute" in sentence containing note 428 with:

an earlier version of this statute

Page 265

Replace Utah paragraph's first sentence with:

Utah Code Ann. § 78B-3-410 (West) allows punitive damages only if compensatory or general damages are awarded.

Page 266

8.10.8 Examples of Punitive Damages Awards in Automobile Fraud Cases

Add to text before first bulleted item:

- *Estate of Overbey v. Chad Franklin National Auto Sales North, L.L.C.*, 361 S.W.3d 364 (Mo. 2012): affirms $500,000 punitive damages award, reduced from $1 million when compensatory damages were $4500, against a car dealer that misrepresented the monthly payment as part of a fraudulent scheme that affected at least thirty-five other buyers.

8.11 Constitutional Limits on Punitive Damages

8.11.1 Overview of the Supreme Court's Decisions on Substantive Limits on Punitive Damages

Page 268

Addition to note 445.

445   *Replace Exxon Shipping Co. v. Baker citation with*: 554 U.S. 471, 128 S. Ct. 2605, 171 L. Ed. 2d 570 (2008) (discussed in § 8.11.3.1, *infra*).

Page 269

Add to text at end of subsection's final paragraph:

The Supreme Court's 2008 decision in *Exxon Shipping Co. v. Baker*[456.1] is discussed in § 8.11.3.1, *infra*.

456.1   554 U.S. 471, 128 S. Ct. 2605, 171 L. Ed. 2d 570 (2008).

8.11.2 Reprehensibility

8.11.2.3 Risks to Health or Safety of Others

Page 270

Addition to note 468.

468   *In re* USA Commercial Mortg. Co., 802 F. Supp. 2d 1147, 1187 (D. Nev. 2011) (risk of harm to others, and the financial vulnerability of these other potential victims, are relevant to reprehensibility).

8.11.2.4 The Vulnerability of the Plaintiff

Page 271

Addition to note 476.

476   *See, e.g., In re* USA Commercial Mortg. Co., 802 F. Supp. 2d 1147, 1187 (D. Nev. 2011) (stressing that many victims were elderly and that their retirement income was at stake).

8.11.2.5 Evidence of Repetition

8.11.2.5.1 Relevance of evidence of repetition

Page 272

Addition to note 487.

487   Estate of Overbey v. Chad Franklin Nat'l Auto Sales N., L.L.C., 361 S.W.3d 364, 374 (Mo. 2012) (fraud was part of a scheme that affected at least thirty-five other consumers).

Page 273

Add new subsection to text after § 8.11.2.6:

8.11.2.7 Reprehensibility When There Are Multiple Claims

Often a case will involve several distinct claims. If the jury awards punitive damages on only one of the claims, a district court held that the court must evaluate reprehensibility based only on the facts of the claim on which punitive damages were awarded.[505.1] How to treat multiple claims when calculating the ratio of punitive damages to compensatory damages is discussed in § 8.11.3.4.4, *infra*.

505.1   Wallace v. Poulos, 861 F. Supp. 2d 587, 604 (D. Md. 2012).

8.11.3 The Ratio of Punitive Damages to Compensatory Damages

8.11.3.1 The Supreme Court's Ratio Rulings

Page 274

8.11.3.1.2 **Exxon Shipping Co. v. Baker** *as interpreting maritime law*

Add to text after second sentence of paragraph containing note 511:

The Court stressed throughout its opinion that its ruling was based on the facts of the particular case,[510.1] and the decision recognizes that higher punitive damages award ratios are appropriate in cases involving smaller damages awards—a principle that the Court has repeatedly stated in its constitutional decisions.[510.2]

510.1   Exxon Shipping Co. v. Baker, 554 U.S. 471, 476, 510–511, 514, 128 S. Ct. 2605, 171 L. Ed. 2d 570 (2008) (framing the issue as "whether the award . . . *in this case* is greater than maritime law should allow *in the circumstances*"; stating that "the upper limit is not directed to cases *like this one*, where the tortious act was worse than negligent but less than malicious"; that "the 3:1 ratio . . . applies to awards in *quite different cases*"; and a 3-to-1 limit is not necessarily reasonable "in this particular type of case"; "anything greater would be excessive *here* and in *cases of this type*" (emphasis added)).

510.2   *Id.*, 554 U.S. at 494.

Addition to note 513.

513   *Replace Duckworth v. United States ex rel. Locke appellate citation with*: 418 Fed. Appx. 2 (D.C. Cir. 2011). *Add: See, e.g.,* In re USA Commercial Mortg. Co., 802 F. Supp. 2d 1147, 1190 n.16 (D. Nev. 2011). *But cf.* Guidance Endodontics, L.L.C. v. Dentsply Int'l, Inc., 791 F. Supp. 2d 1026 (D.N.M. 2011) (concluding that, while *Gore* rather than *Baker* controls non-maritime cases, *Baker*'s reasoning should still be considered, and the Supreme Court is likely to impose bright-line 1-to-1 ratio).

Add to text at end of subsection:

Even in maritime cases, courts facing different facts are likely to find the one-to-one limit inapplicable.[513.1]

513.1   *See, e.g.,* Clausen v. Icicle Seafoods, Inc., 272 P.3d 827 (Wash. 2012) (confining *Exxon* to its facts; not binding when defendant's acts were callous, willful, and wanton rather than merely reckless).

Page 275

8.11.3.2 Justifying a High Ratio

Addition to notes 521, 523, 526, 527.

521   Estate of Overbey v. Chad Franklin Nat'l Auto Sales N., L.L.C., 361 S.W.3d 364 (Mo. 2012) (upholding $500,000 punitive damages for automobile finance fraud when compensatory damages were $4500, a 111-to-1 ratio; while harm was economic, target was financially vulnerable, and the fraud was intentional and part of a scheme that harmed others).

Page 277

523   Arizona Dep't of Law Civil Rights Div. v. ASARCO, L.L.C., 798 F. Supp. 2d 1023 (D. Ariz. 2011) (finding $868,750 punitive damages award not to be excessive when compensatory damages for sexual harassment by defendant's employee were $1; reducing award to $300,000 because of Title VII cap on damages); Howard Univ. v. Wilkins, 22 A.3d 774 (D.C. 2011) (affirming $42,677.50 punitive damages award when compensatory damages were $1); *cf.* Wallace v. Poulos, 861 F. Supp. 2d 587 (D. Md. 2012) (higher ratio is allowable when compensatory damages are nominal but here, because evidence of reprehensibility is mixed, $500,000 punitive damages award must be reduced to $20,000 for plaintiff whose compensatory damages are $1, and $2.5 million punitive damages award must be reduced to $125,000 for plaintiff whose compensatory damages are $3000).

Page 278

526   Arnold v. Wilder, 657 F.3d 353 (6th Cir. 2011) (reinstating $550,000 of jury's punitive damages award, which trial court had reduced to $229,600, when compensatory damages for police assault were $57,400, a 9.5-to-1 ratio).

Page 279

527   *See, e.g.,* Ondrisek v. Hoffman, 698 F.3d 1020 (8th Cir. 2012) (4-to-1 ratio is constitutional maximum when compensatory damages are $3 million, despite exceptionally reprehensible conduct); Payne v. Jones, 696 F.3d 189 (2d Cir. 2012) (reducing punitive damages award to 1.7-to-1 when court perceives evidence of reprehensibility as mixed and punitive damages awards it approved in similar cases were smaller); Jones v. United Parcel Serv., Inc., 674 F.3d 1187 (10th Cir. 2012) (ratio of 3.17-to-1 is constitutionally excessive when compensatory damages for wrongful termination of employment were substantial ($630,307); requiring reduction to 1-to-1); Guidance Endodontics, L.L.C. v. Dentsply Int'l, Inc., 791 F. Supp. 2d 1026 (D.N.M. 2011) (giving weight to Exxon Shipping Co. v. Baker, 554 U.S. 471 (2008), and limiting punitive damages award to 1-to-1 ratio when compensatory damages were over $1 million).

Page 280

8.11.3.3 Increasing the Ratio When Previous Awards Have Not Achieved Deterrence

Addition to notes 531, 532.

531   *See, e.g.,* Neuros Co., Ltd. v. KTurbo, Inc., 698 F.3d 514, 520 (7th Cir. 2012) (stating in *dicta* that trial court should have awarded more than $50,000 in punitive damages to achieve deterrence).

532   *See* Arizona Dep't of Law Civil Rights Div. v. ASARCO, L.L.C., 798 F. Supp. 2d 1023, 1048–1049 (D. Ariz. 2011) (large punitive damages award is necessary to deter large company that failed to address repeated sexual harassment of employee).

8.11.3.4 Including All Actual and Potential Harm to the Plaintiff in the Ratio

Page 282

8.11.3.4.2 What can be included in the compensatory damages award to which punitive damages are compared?

Addition to notes 552, 555.

552   *In re* USA Commercial Mortg. Co., 802 F. Supp. 2d 1147, 1188–1189 (D. Nev. 2011).

555   *See also In re* USA Commercial Mortg. Co., 802 F. Supp. 2d 1147, 1188–1189 (D. Nev. 2011) (prejudgment interest, costs, and attorney fees should be included); Guidance Endodontics, L.L.C. v. Dentsply Int'l, Inc., 791 F. Supp. 2d 1026 (D.N.M. 2011) (legal costs can be considered in addition to compensatory damages when evaluating whether punitive damages award is excessive); Clausen v. Icicle Seafoods, Inc., 272 P.3d 827, 836 (Wash. 2012) (attorney fees plaintiff incurred to enforce right to payment of living expenses and medical expenses caused by maritime injury are to be included in compensatory award for purposes of calculating ratio).

Page 285

8.11.3.4.5 Using the right ratio for the right defendant

Addition to notes 577, 580.

577   *Accord In re* USA Commercial Mortg. Co., 802 F. Supp. 2d 1147, 1189 (D. Nev. 2011).

580   *But cf. In re* USA Commercial Mortg. Co., 802 F. Supp. 2d 1147, 1189 (D. Nev. 2011) (aggregating all compensatory damages awards for all plaintiffs when jury did not make plaintiff-by-plaintiff awards).

8.11.4 Presenting Evidence of Other Penalties for the Specific Conduct at Issue

Page 287

8.11.4.2 Comparable Penalties in Automobile Fraud Cases

Addition to notes 595, 598, 602, 604.

595   *Replace NCLC UDAP citation with*: National Consumer Law Center, Unfair and Deceptive Acts and Practices §§ 12.4.1, 13.5 (8th ed. 2012).

598   *Replace NCLC UDAP citation with*: National Consumer Law Center, Unfair and Deceptive Acts and Practices §§ 12.4.1, 13.5 (8th ed. 2012).

602   *See In re* USA Commercial Mortg. Co., 802 F. Supp. 2d 1147, 1191 (D. Nev. 2011) (using Nevada's punitive damages cap as comparison); Arizona Dep't of Law Civil Rights Div. v. ASARCO, L.L.C., 798 F. Supp. 2d 1023, 1044 (D. Ariz. 2011) ($300,000 statutory cap on Title VII damages is appropriate comparison).

Page 288

604   Davis v. Rennie, 264 F.3d 86, 117 (1st Cir. 2001); *see also* Payne v. Jones, 696 F.3d 189 (2d Cir. 2012) (reducing punitive damages award to be consistent with awards in similar cases).

Page 289

8.11.5 Presenting Evidence of Defendant's Wealth When Appropriate

Addition to note 616.

616   Wallace v. Poulos, 861 F. Supp. 2d 587, 600–601 (D. Md. 2012); Guidance Endodontics, L.L.C. v. Dentsply Int'l, Inc., 791 F. Supp. 2d 1026 (D.N.M. 2011).

Page 291

8.11.6 Framing Jury Instructions

Replace note 628 with:

628   *See* § 8.11.3.4.4, *supra.*

Add to text after sentence containing note 628:

If the jury misapprehends the instructions and renders a verdict that finds liability on two similar claims but awards damages on only one, it may be necessary to make an objection before the jury is discharged. There is a risk in making such an objection though, because sending the jury back for further deliberations places the favorable part of the verdict as well as the unfavorable part at risk. The court may be willing to treat damages the jury awards on one count as applicable to other counts,[628.1] but the consumer's position is stronger if the jury states the amount of damages applicable to each count.

628.1   *See* Bird v. John Chezik Homerun, Inc., 152 F.3d 1014, 1016–1017 (8th Cir. 1998) ("The only plausible explanation for the jury's failure to award damages on Count II is that the jury had already awarded Bird damages on Count I for essentially the same conduct and did not want to award her the same damages twice.").

Page 292

Add new subsection to text
after § 8.11.7:

8.11.8 Gore *Standards Do Not Limit Statutory or Multiple Damages*

8.11.8.1 Introduction

The Supreme Court's decisions in such cases as *BMW of North America, Inc. v. Gore*,[636.1] *State Farm Mutual Automobile Insurance Co. v. Campbell*,[636.2] and *Phillip Morris USA v. Williams*,[636.3] discussed in the preceding subsections, require courts to evaluate punitive damages awards against three guideposts: the degree of reprehensibility; the ratio between punitive and compensatory damages; and a comparison to the penalties authorized or imposed in comparable cases.[636.4]

While punitive damages are available in most jurisdictions for fraud and other intentional torts, the statutory or multiple damages that are available under many consumer protection laws can also provide a substantial recovery for the consumer and deter fraudulent behavior. For example, many UDAP statutes allow statutory or multiple damages.[636.5] The typical state odometer statute allows statutory damages, often $1500 or $2500,[636.6] and the federal odometer statute now provides for statutory damages of $10,000.[636.7] As detailed in the subsections that follow, there are strong arguments that the Supreme Court's punitive damages guideposts do not apply to statutory and multiple damages.

8.11.8.2 The Supreme Court Has Upheld the Constitutionality of Statutory Damages Without Regard to Their Ratio to Actual Harm

The only time the United States Supreme Court has addressed the constitutionality of statutory damages is in its 1919 decision *St. Louis, Iron Mountain & Southern Railway Co. v. Williams*.[636.8] The Court there addressed an Arkansas statute that imposed a penalty of between $50 and $300 on railroads that charged more than the fare approved by law. The appellant railroad had collected 66¢ more than the authorized fare. The lower court awarded the passenger the 66¢ overcharge, plus a penalty of $75—a ratio of 113-to-1 to the 66¢ compensatory award.

The Court rejected the railroad's argument that the penalty denied the railroad due process because it was arbitrary and unreasonable, and not proportionate to the actual damages sustained. The penalty did not have to be proportionate to the aggrieved passenger's loss even though it was to be awarded to the passenger rather than to the state. Because the purpose of the law was to secure adherence to the rate structure, the legislature was free to key the amount to the public wrong done rather than to the private injury. Therefore, the validity of the penalty was to be considered in light of "the interests of the public, the numberless opportunities for committing the offense, and the need for securing uniform adherence to established passenger rates."[636.9] This holding represents a specific rejection of the Court's position in *Philip Morris* that harm to others can only be considered in determining how reprehensible the defendant's acts were, not in determining the ratio between compensatory and punitive damages.[636.10]

The Court concluded that statutory damages violate due process only if they are "so severe and oppressive as to be wholly disproportioned to the offense and obviously unreasonable."[636.11] While this standard incorporates some element of proportionality, the requirement that the penalty be "wholly" disproportionate *and* "obviously" unreasonable gives far greater weight to the legislative judgment than *Gore* and *State Farm* give to jury determinations. Notably, the Court did not list either of the other *Gore* guideposts—reprehensibility and comparability to other penalties—as factors. Indeed, the Court stressed that states "possess a wide latitude of discretion" in setting statutory damages.[636.12] While the Supreme Court's decision deals with statutory damages, its rationale would apply equally to multiple damages, such as the treble damages provisions of many UDAP statutes.

In line with the Supreme Court's decision, many courts have upheld statutory or multiple damages awards, and have held that they are not subject to the *Gore/State Farm* standards.[636.13]

636.1 517 U.S. 559, 116 S. Ct. 1589, 134 L. Ed. 2d 809 (1996).
636.2 538 U.S. 408, 123 S. Ct. 1513, 155 L. Ed. 2d 585 (2003).
636.3 549 U.S. 346, 127 S. Ct. 1057, 166 L. Ed. 2d 940 (2007).
636.4 *Gore*, 517 U.S. at 575.
636.5 *See* § 9.4.10, *infra*.
636.6 *See* Appx. C, *infra*.
636.7 *See* § 6.8.2.1, *supra*.
636.8 251 U.S. 63, 40 S. Ct. 71, 64 L. Ed. 139 (1919).

636.9 *Id.*, 251 U.S. at 67.
636.10 *See* § 8.11.1, *supra*.
636.11 *Williams*, 251 U.S. at 67.
636.12 *Williams*, 251 U.S. at 66.
636.13 *See, e.g.*, Matamoros v. Starbucks Corp., 699 F.3d 129 (1st Cir. 2012); Capitol Records, Inc. v. Thomas-Rasset, 692 F.3d 899 (8th Cir. 2012), *petition for cert. filed*, 81 U.S.L.W. 3348 (Dec. 10, 2012); United States v. Bourseau, 2006 WL 3949169, at *2 (S.D. Cal. Dec. 1, 2006), *aff'd on other grounds*, 531 F.3d 1159 (9th Cir. 2008); Accounting Outsourcing, L.L.C. v. Verizon Wireless Personal Communications, Ltd. P'ship, 329 F. Supp. 2d 789, 808–809 (M.D. La. 2004); Lowry's Reports, Inc. v. Legg Mason, Inc., 302 F. Supp. 2d 455, 460 (D. Md. 2004); Kenro, Inc. v. Fax Daily, Inc., 962 F. Supp. 1162, 1165 (S.D. Ind. 1997); *In re* Marriage of Chen & Ulner, 820 N.E.2d 1136, 1152 (Ill. App. Ct. 2004); *see also* Zomba Enterprises, Inc. v. Panorama Records, Inc., 491 F.3d 574, 586–587 (6th Cir. 2007); *In re* Marriage of Miller, 879 N.E.2d 292 (Ill. 2007) ($100/day statutory damages for failing to withhold child support from employee's pay, totaling $1,172,100, does not violate substantive due process).

As discussed below, the key concerns that underlie the Supreme Court's decisions in *Gore* and *State Farm* are simply not present in the case of statutory and multiple damages.

8.11.8.3 Fair Notice Is Provided by Statutory Damage Provisions

One of the concerns underlying *Gore's* punitive damages ruling is that: "Elementary notions of fairness enshrined in our constitutional jurisprudence dictate that a person receive *fair notice* not only of the conduct that will subject him to punishment, but also of the severity of the penalty that a State may impose."[636.14] By contrast, fair notice is not an issue in the case of statutory or multiple damages, because the statute itself provides full and fair notice of the potential severity of the penalty.

For example, the Eighth Circuit's 2012 decision in *Capitol Records, Inc. v. Thomas-Rasset*[636.15] holds that a statutory damages award of $222,000 made pursuant to the Copyright Act did not violate due process, because concerns regarding fair notice are simply not applicable in cases involving statutory damages.[636.16] The damages award was derived from multiplying the number of copyrighted works (24) that had been willfully infringed by $9250, a figure that fell within the penalty-per-work range of $750 to $150,000 that is provided in the Copyright Act. The court held that the district court erred concluding that $2250 per work, for a total of $54,000, was the maximum permitted by the Constitution.

In reaching this conclusion the Eighth Circuit specifically rejected the defendant's plea that it apply the *Gore/State Farm* guideposts in order to address the issue of due process. Noting that a primary concern of due process is fair notice of the conduct that will subject a defendant to punishment and of the severity of the penalty, the court stated that "[t]his concern about fair notice does not apply to statutory damages, because those damages are identified and constrained by the authorizing statute."[636.17] Thus, rather than applying the *Gore/State Farm* guideposts, the court applied the standard stated in the Supreme Court's 1919 *Williams* decision that damages awarded pursuant to a statute violate due process only if they are "so severe and

oppressive as to be wholly disproportioned to the offense and obviously unreasonable."[636.18] Reiterating that case's pronouncement that Congress possesses a "wide latitude of discretion"[636.19] in setting statutory damages under this standard, and pointing out that the award was "toward the lower end" of the broad range of statutory damages established by Congress under its "wide latitude of discretion" in setting such damages, the court in *Capitol Records* found that the $222,000 award was not "so severe or oppressive" under the circumstances as to warrant any reduction.[636.20]

8.11.8.4 Comparison of Actual Harm to Punitive Damages May Be Impossible

Another major reason cited by the Eighth Circuit in *Capitol Records* for refusing to apply the *Gore/State Farm* criteria to statutory damages is that the second guidepost—that of comparing actual harm suffered to the punitive damages imposed—has no logical application in cases involving statutory damages. Because statutory damages are often crafted for instances in which actual harm cannot be determined, any comparison between the harm actually suffered and the statutory damages awarded is by definition infeasible. As *Capitol Records* opines, the application of the *Gore/State Farm* guideposts "would be nonsensical if applied to statutory damages" as "[i]t makes no sense to consider the disparity between 'actual harm' and an award of statutory damages when statutory damages are designed precisely for instances where actual harm is difficult or impossible to calculate."[636.21]

8.11.8.5 Many Statutory and Multiple Damages Provisions Are Compensatory Rather Than Punitive in Nature

A third reason that the *Gore/State Farm* guideposts are irrelevant to statutory and multiple damages is that many such provisions are intended to be compensatory rather than punitive in nature. For example, the Massachusetts Wage Act explicitly states that its treble damages provision represents liquidated damages.[636.22] In *Matamoros v. Starbucks Corp.*[636.23] the First Circuit held that, because a treble damages award under this statute "is neither an award of punitive damages nor fairly analogous to such an award," the *Gore/State Farm* criteria did

---

636.14 BMW of N. Am., Inc. v. Gore, 517 U.S. 559, 560, 116 S. Ct. 1589, 134 L. Ed. 2d 809 (1996) (emphasis added).

636.15 692 F.3d 899 (8th Cir. 2012), *petition for cert. filed*, 81 U.S.L.W. 3348 (Dec. 10, 2012).

636.16 *Accord* Accounting Outsourcing, L.L.C. v. Verizon Wireless Personal Communications, Ltd. P'ship, 329 F. Supp. 2d 789, 808–809 (M.D. La. 2004) (upholding junk facsimile statutory damages provision); *In re* Marriage of Chen & Ulner, 820 N.E.2d 1136, 1152 (Ill. App. Ct. 2004).

636.17 Capitol Records, Inc. v. Thomas-Rasset, 692 F.3d 899, 907 (8th Cir. 2012), *petition for cert. filed*, 81 U.S.L.W. 3348 (Dec. 10, 2012); *accord* Lowry's Reports, Inc. v. Legg Mason, Inc., 302 F. Supp. 2d 455, 460 (D. Md. 2004) (because "statutory damages are limited to certain specific circumstances," the "unregulated and arbitrary use of judicial power that the *Gore* guideposts remedy is not implicated in Congress' carefully crafted and reasonably constrained [copyright] statute").

636.18 St. Louis, Iron Mtn. & S. Ry. Co. v. Williams, 251 U.S. 63, 67, 40 S. Ct. 71, 64 L. Ed. 139 (1919).

636.19 *Id.*, 251 U.S. at 66.

636.20 *Capitol Records*, 692 F.3d at 908.

636.21 *Id.* at 907; *see also* Lowry's Reports, Inc. v. Legg Mason, Inc., 302 F. Supp. 2d 455, 460 (D. Md. 2004) ("The *Gore* guideposts do not limit the statutory damages here because of the difficulties in assessing compensatory damages in this case.... Statutory damages exist in part because of the difficulties in proving—and providing compensation for—actual harm in copyright infringement actions.").

636.22 Mass. Gen. Laws ch. 149, § 150.

636.23 699 F.3d 129 (1st Cir. 2012).

not apply, and the defendant's concerns regarding due process were "misplaced."[636.24]

8.11.8.6 Statutory Damages Are Not Decided in an "Imprecise Manner"

Another key concern of the Supreme Court in *Gore* was "the imprecise manner in which punitive damages systems are administered."[636.25] This concern is also not relevant to statu-

tory or multiple damages.[636.26] As the First Circuit held in *Matamoros*: "Here—unlike in [*State Farm Mutual Automobile Ins. v.*] *Campbell*—there is no cause for concern about the 'imprecise manner in which punitive damages systems are administered' by juries. . . . To the contrary, the current treble damages provision in the Massachusetts Wage Act reflects a reasoned legislative judgment. This is an important distinction."[636.27]

636.24 *Id.* at 140; *see also* Morse Diesel Int'l, Inc. v. United States, 79 Fed. Cl. 116, 126 (Fed. Cl. 2007) (penalties and treble damages under False Claims Act have a compensatory side; *State Farm* inapplicable); United States v. Bourseau, 2006 WL 3949169, at *2 (S.D. Cal. Dec. 1, 2006) (rejecting argument that treble damages award violated *State Farm* "in view of the mixed compensatory and punitive nature of False Claims Act treble damages"), *aff'd on other grounds*, 531 F.3d 1159 (9th Cir. 2008); Vader v. Fleetwood Enterprises, Inc., 201 P.3d 139 (Mont. 2009) (rejecting *Gore* objections to double damages award under state UDAP statute; multiple UDAP damages are remedial, not punitive in nature); *cf.* F.C. Bloxom Co. v. Fireman's Fund Ins. Co., 2012 WL 5992286, at *7–8 (W.D. Wash. Nov. 30, 2012) (questioning whether treble damages provision of state unfair insurance practices act is punitive, but even if it is, unreasonable acts are sufficiently reprehensible to justify an award).

636.25 State Farm Mut. Auto. Ins. Co. v. Campbell, 538 U.S. 408, 417, 123 S. Ct. 1513, 155 L. Ed. 2d 585 (2003).

636.26 Matamoros v. Starbucks Corp., 699 F.3d 129 (1st Cir. 2012).

636.27 *Id.* at 140; *accord* Morse Diesel Int'l, Inc. v. United States, 79 Fed. Cl. 116, 126 (Fed. Cl. 2007) (*State Farm* balancing test inapplicable to penalties and treble damages under False Claims Act; no concern about imprecision or subjectivity because "Congress, not a jury, has prescribed a civil penalty range and mandated the imposition of treble damages"); United States v. Bourseau, 2006 WL 3949169, at *2 (S.D. Cal. Dec. 1, 2006) (rejecting argument that treble damages award violated *State Farm*, as it was "not the product of a jury verdict and does not have the potentially arbitrary quality of a classic punitive damages award"), *aff'd on other grounds*, 531 F.3d 1159 (9th Cir. 2008); *In re* Marriage of Chen & Ulner, 820 N.E.2d 1136, 1152 (Ill. App. Ct. 2004) ("Stated simply, the concerns over the imprecise manner in which punitive damages systems are administered are not present here. Unlike the inherent uncertainty associated with punitive damages, section 35 of the [Income Withholding for] Support Act provides employers with exact notice of the $100-per-day penalty they will face for failing to comply with a support order.").

Chapter 9

Warranty, Mistake, UDAP, RICO, Unconscionability, and Negligence Claims

Page 295

9.1 Introduction

Addition to note 1.

   1   *Replace NCLC UDAP citation with*: National Consumer Law Center, Unfair and Deceptive Acts and Practices (8th ed. 2012).

9.2 Warranty Claims

9.2.2 Dealer's Breach of Warranty of Title

Page 297

9.2.2.1 Nature of Warranty of Title

Addition to note 21.

   21   *See also* Super., Inc. v. Arrington, 70 U.C.C. Rep. Serv. 2d 919 (Ark. Ct. App. 2009) (enforcing trade usage that motor vehicle dealer will reimburse buyer if title is challenged, even if buyer might be able to defend title as good faith purchaser).

9.2.3 Express Warranties

Page 303

9.2.3.3 Disclaimers and Parol Evidence

Addition to note 93.

   93   *See, e.g.*, Epsman v. Martin-Landers, L.L.C., 64 U.C.C. Rep. Serv. 2d 19 (E.D. Ark. 2007) (statement in Buyers Guide that all repairs are buyer's responsibility does not negate express warranty that vehicle's mileage was 106,550).

9.2.4 Implied Warranties

Page 305

9.2.4.2 Implied Warranties in Automobile Fraud Cases

Addition to note 115.

  115   *But cf.* Jones v. Koons Auto., Inc., 752 F. Supp. 2d 670, 685 (D. Md. 2010) (failure to disclose car's history as short term rental is not breach of implied warranty of merchantability); Paulk v. Thomasville Ford Lincoln Mercury, Inc., 732 S.E.2d 297 (Ga. Ct. App. 2012) (rebuilt wreck for which dealer paid substantial price, and which consumers drove for 24,000 miles, passes without objection in the trade, when consumers' problems with car were unrelated to the wreck damage).

Add to text after sentence containing note 116:

     This aspect of the implied warranty of merchantability is a means of enforcing the contract description, and thus is similar to an express warranty. It is particularly significant because failure to comply with an implied warranty, as defined by state law, is a violation of the Magnuson-Moss Act, which allows recovery of attorney fees.[116.1] Thus, when a vehicle does not conform to its contract description, that breaches the implied warranty of merchantability and is actionable under the Magnuson-Moss Act.

  116.1   *See* § 9.2.11, *infra*.

9.2.7 Revocation of Acceptance As a UCC Remedy

Page 309

9.2.7.2 When May a Consumer Revoke Acceptance?

Add note 163.1 at end of subsection's third bulleted item.

  163.1   *Cf.* Paulk v. Thomasville Ford Lincoln Mercury, Inc., 732 S.E.2d 297 (Ga. Ct. App. 2012) (refusing revocation when buyer saw and asked about signs of repaired damage before sale yet went through with sale and did not revoke acceptance until much later).

9.2.11 Application of Magnuson-Moss Warranty Act to Automobile Fraud Claims

Page 317

9.2.11.3 Implied Warranty Claims Under the Magnuson-Moss Warranty Act

Replace "in the trade" in sentence containing note 232 with:

in the trade under the contract description

Add to text at end of subsection's second paragraph:

Nonconformity with the contract description is thus a breach of the implied warranty of merchantability and is actionable as a Magnuson-Moss violation even though the contract description would not meet the Magnuson-Moss definition of "express warranty."[232.1]

232.1   *See* § 9.2.11.2, *supra*.

9.3 Mistake

Page 318

9.3.1 Benefits of a Claim of Mistake

Replace note 246 with:

246   *See* § 9.4.10, *infra*; National Consumer Law Center, Unfair and Deceptive Acts and Practices § 12.8 (8th ed. 2012).

Page 319

9.3.2 Elements of a Claim of Mistake

Addition to note 259.

259   *See* Mickelsen v. Broadway Ford, Inc., 280 P.3d 176 (Idaho 2012) (denying relief when mistake was only on buyer's part).

9.4 UDAP Claims

9.4.1 Advantages and Disadvantages in Automobile Fraud Cases

9.4.1.1 Strengths and Benefits of UDAP Claims

Addition to note 268.

268   *Replace NCLC UDAP citation with*: National Consumer Law Center, Unfair and Deceptive Acts and Practices Appx. A (8th ed. 2012).

Page 320

Replace note 269 with:

269   *See* National Consumer Law Center, Unfair and Deceptive Acts and Practices § 4.2.15.1 (8th ed. 2012).

9.4.1.2 Comparison to Warranty Claims

Replace note 273 with:

273   National Consumer Law Center, Unfair and Deceptive Acts and Practices § 4.2.19 (8th ed. 2012).

9.4.1.3 Disadvantages of UDAP Claims

Replace note 275 with:

275   *See* § 9.4.9, *infra*; National Consumer Law Center, Unfair and Deceptive Acts and Practices § 11.4.4 (8th ed. 2012).

Addition to note 276.

276   *See* § 9.4.9, *infra. See generally* National Consumer Law Center, Unfair and Deceptive Acts and Practices § 11.4.3 (8th ed. 2012).

9.4.1.4 Combining UDAP Claims with Other Claims

Replace note 278 with:

278   *See* National Consumer Law Center, Unfair and Deceptive Acts and Practices §§ 12.3.7, 12.4.2.6, 12.4.3.8 (8th ed. 2012).

Page 321

9.4.1.5 Misrepresentation Claim Under Federal Odometer Statute As Alternative to UDAP Claim

Replace sentence containing note 285 with:

MVICSA remedies include mandatory treble damages or $10,000,[285] whichever is greater.

285   *See* § 6.8.2, *supra.*

9.4.2 Scope Issues

Replace notes 286, 288, 290 with:

286   *See* National Consumer Law Center, Unfair and Deceptive Acts and Practices §§ 12.3.7, 12.4.2.6, 12.4.3.8 (8th ed. 2012).

288   *See* National Consumer Law Center, Unfair and Deceptive Acts and Practices §§ 2.3.1, 2.3.3 (8th ed. 2012).

290   National Consumer Law Center, Unfair and Deceptive Acts and Practices § 2.2.1.6 (8th ed. 2012).

Addition to note 291.

291   *Replace NCLC UDAP citation with*: National Consumer Law Center, Unfair and Deceptive Acts and Practices §§ 2.3.8, 4.2.19.3 (8th ed. 2012).
       Add: *See, e.g.*, Branin v. TMC Enterprises, L.L.C., 832 F. Supp. 2d 646 (W.D. Va. 2011) (UDAP statute applies to prior dealer in chain of title who knew that car was likely to be resold to a consumer, but does not apply to prior dealer's employee).

Page 322

9.4.3 Deception Standard

Addition to notes 293, 294.

293   *Replace NCLC UDAP citation with*: National Consumer Law Center, Unfair and Deceptive Acts and Practices § 4.2.4 (8th ed. 2012).

294   *Replace NCLC UDAP citation with*: National Consumer Law Center, Unfair and Deceptive Acts and Practices § 4.2.5 (8th ed. 2012).
       Add: *See* Gregory v. Poulin Auto Sales, Inc., 44 A.3d 788 (Vt. 2012) (dealer's unknowing misrepresentation that vehicle's title was clear and odometer reading accurate is UDAP violation).

Replace note 295 with:

295   National Consumer Law Center, Unfair and Deceptive Acts and Practices § 4.2.6 (8th ed. 2012).

Add to text at end of subsection's first paragraph:

The consumer's failure to conduct an independent investigation of the vehicle's history is not a defense.[299.1]

299.1   Gregory v. Poulin Auto Sales, Inc., 44 A.3d 788 (Vt. 2012).

Replace notes 300, 302 with:
Page 323

300   National Consumer Law Center, Unfair and Deceptive Acts and Practices § 4.2.19 (8th ed. 2012).

302   *See* National Consumer Law Center, Unfair and Deceptive Acts and Practices § 4.2.19.2 (8th ed. 2012).

9.4.4 Failure to Disclose As Deceptive

Addition to notes 308, 310.

308   *Replace NCLC UDAP citation with*: National Consumer Law Center, Unfair and Deceptive Acts and Practices Appx. A (8th ed. 2012).

310   *Replace NCLC UDAP citation with*: National Consumer Law Center, Unfair and Deceptive Acts and Practices § 4.2.14 (8th ed. 2012).

Page 324

Replace note 312 with:

312   *See* National Consumer Law Center, Unfair and Deceptive Acts and Practices § 4.2.13 (8th ed. 2012).

Addition to notes 313, 316, 317.

313   *Replace NCLC UDAP citation with*: National Consumer Law Center, Unfair and Deceptive Acts and Practices § 4.2.13 (8th ed. 2012).

316   *Replace NCLC UDAP citation with*: National Consumer Law Center, Unfair and Deceptive Acts and Practices § 4.2.12.4 (8th ed. 2012).

317   *Replace NCLC UDAP citation with*: National Consumer Law Center, Unfair and Deceptive Acts and Practices §§ 4.2.14.3.5–4.2.14.3.7 (8th ed. 2012).

9.4.5 Unfairness and Unconscionability

9.4.5.1 Unfairness

Replace notes 319, 322 with:
Page 325

319   National Consumer Law Center, Unfair and Deceptive Acts and Practices Appx. A (8th ed. 2012).

322   National Consumer Law Center, Unfair and Deceptive Acts and Practices § 4.3.3.3 (8th ed. 2012).

9.4.5.2 Unconscionability

Addition to note 324.

324   *Replace NCLC UDAP citation with*: National Consumer Law Center, Unfair and Deceptive Acts and Practices (8th ed. 2012).

9.4.6 Violation of Another Statute

Page 326

9.4.6.1 Introduction

Replace note 330 with:

330   National Consumer Law Center, Unfair and Deceptive Acts and Practices § 3.2.7.3 (8th ed. 2012).

Page 327

9.4.6.2 Precedent Finding Statutory Violations to Be Automatic UDAP Violations

Replace note 350 with:

350   National Consumer Law Center, Unfair and Deceptive Acts and Practices § 5.6.7.1 (8th ed. 2012).

Addition to notes 352, 353.

352   *Add to In re Kehauoha-Alisa citation*: *rev'd*, 674 F.3d 1083 (9th Cir. 2012) (not adopting per se approach, but reversing on basis that bankruptcy appellate panel erred in finding only technical violation of statute that required strict compliance with public announcement of foreclosure sale, and in not affording relief under that disclosure statute).

353   *Replace Perez v. Nidek Co. Ltd. citation with*: 657 F. Supp. 2d 1156 (S.D. Cal. 2009).

Page 328

9.4.6.3 Arguing That a Statutory Violation Is a Per Se UDAP Violation

Addition to note 358.

358   *Replace NCLC UDAP citation with*: National Consumer Law Center, Unfair and Deceptive Acts and Practices § 3.2.7.4.2 (8th ed. 2012).

9.4.8 Application of UDAP Standards to Automobile Fraud Cases

Page 329

9.4.8.1 Odometer Rollbacks and Mileage Misrepresentations

Addition to notes 363, 364.

363   *VIRGINIA*: Branin v. TMC Enterprises, L.L.C., 832 F. Supp. 2d 646 (W.D. Va. 2011) (UDAP statute applicable to prior dealer in chain of title who falsely certified odometer reading as accurate).

Page 330

364   Gregory v. Poulin Auto Sales, Inc., 44 A.3d 788 (Vt. 2012) (dealer's false statement that odometer reading was accurate is UDAP violation even though dealer did not know the truth).

9.4.8.2 Salvage and Collision History

Addition to notes 365, 366.

365   *GEORGIA*: *But cf.* Isbell v. Credit Nation Lending Serv., L.L.C., 735 S.E.2d 46 (Ga. Ct. App. 2012) (denying UDAP claim on ground that consumers did not exercise due diligence when they proceeded with purchase without waiting for seller to respond to request for vehicle history report, and did not have car inspected even though they were warned it might have a bent frame); Paulk v. Thomasville Ford Lincoln Mercury, Inc., 732 S.E.2d 297 (Ga. Ct. App. 2012) (salesperson's statement that he was not sure about vehicle's history was not UDAP violation when Carfax report did not show accident, even though consumer's expert testified that damage would be obvious to anyone in used car business).
      VERMONT: Gregory v. Poulin Auto Sales, Inc., 44 A.3d 788 (Vt. 2012) (dealer's unknowing misrepresentation that vehicle title was clean is UDAP violation).

Page 331

366   Gregory v. Poulin Auto Sales, Inc., 44 A.3d 788 (Vt. 2012) (dealer's false statement that vehicle's title was clean is UDAP violation even though dealer did not know the truth).

Page 332

Add to text after sentence containing note 373:

Undisclosed damage may also lead indirectly to other UDAP violations. For example, it is a UDAP violation to represent that a vehicle comes with a manufacturer's warranty or is eligible for a service contract when wreck damage makes it ineligible for coverage.[373.1]

373.1   *See, e.g.*, Gionis v. Russo's Marine Mart, Inc., 2012 WL 6582617 (Conn. Super. Ct. Nov. 19, 2012) (undisclosed damage to boat had voided warranty). *See generally* National Consumer Law Center, Consumer Warranty Law §§ 11.1.6, 11.1.7 (4th ed. 2010 and Supp.).

9.4.8.3 Lemon Laundering and Nondisclosure of History of Mechanical Problems

Replace notes 376, 377 with:

376 *See* § 9.4.2, *supra. See generally* National Consumer Law Center, *Unfair and Deceptive Acts and Practices* § 4.2.19 (8th ed. 2012).

377 National Consumer Law Center, *Unfair and Deceptive Acts and Practices* §§ 4.2.4, 4.2.5 (8th ed. 2012).

Page 334

9.4.8.4 Nature of Prior Use

Addition to note 392.

392 *CALIFORNIA*: Whited v. Galindo (*In re* Galindo), 467 B.R. 201, 209 (Bankr. S.D. Cal. 2012) (misrepresentation that daily rental car had been owned by salesman's friend violations California Consumers Legal Remedies Act).
  ILLINOIS: *See also* Mulderink v. RSB Enterprises, Inc., 2012 WL 3151384 (N.D. Ill. Aug. 2, 2012) (finding UDAP violation when dealer, knowing that consumer did not want to buy a vehicle purchased at a particular auction, misrepresented that vehicle had not been purchased there).

9.4.8.5 Sale of Used Cars As New

Page 336

9.4.8.5.1 Deceptive to represent used cars as new

Addition to note 403.

403 *CALIFORNIA*: *Add at end of Bourgi v. W. Covina Motors, Inc. citation*: *later opinion at* 2011 WL 2207477 (Cal. Ct. App. June 8, 2011) (unpublished) (affirming judgment against consumer).
  OHIO: *But see* Olah v. Ganley Chevrolet, Inc., 946 N.E.2d 771 (Ohio Ct. App. 2010) (parol evidence rule bars claim that seller committed fraud and UDAP violation by representing vehicle as new, when contract stated it was used).

Page 340

9.4.9 Limitations on UDAP Litigation

Replace note 440 with:

440 *See* National Consumer Law Center, *Unfair and Deceptive Acts and Practices* § 11.4.2 (8th ed. 2012).

Addition to note 442.

442 *Replace NCLC UDAP citation with*: National Consumer Law Center, *Unfair and Deceptive Acts and Practices* § 11.4.4 (8th ed. 2012).

Replace notes 444, 445, 453 with:

444 *See* National Consumer Law Center, *Unfair and Deceptive Acts and Practices* § 11.4.4 (8th ed. 2012).

445 *Id.* § 11.4.3.

Page 341

453 *See* National Consumer Law Center, *Unfair and Deceptive Acts and Practices* § 11.2 (8th ed. 2012).

9.4.10 UDAP Remedies

Replace notes 454, 455 with:

454 *Id.* § 12.3.2.
455 *Id.* § 12.3.3.

Addition to note 456.

456 *Replace "Id.* § 13.4.2." *with*: *Id.* § 12.4.2.

Add to text after sentence containing note 456:

Courts generally hold that the constitutional limits on punitive damages announced by the Supreme Court[456.1] do not apply to statutory multiple damages.[456.2]

456.1 *See* § 8.11, *supra.*
456.2 *See* National Consumer Law Center, *Unfair and Deceptive Acts and Practices* § 11.9.4 (8th ed. 2012).

Replace note 457 with:

457 *See* National Consumer Law Center, *Unfair and Deceptive Acts and Practices* § 12.4.1 (8th ed. 2012).

Add to text after sentence containing note 458:

Significantly, there is strong authority that the Supreme Court's limits on punitive damages do not apply to multiple damages and minimum damages set by a statute.[458.1]

458.1 *See* § 8.11.8 (Supp.), *supra.*

Replace note 460 with:

460 *See* National Consumer Law Center, *Unfair and Deceptive Acts and Practices* § 12.4.1.4 (8th ed. 2012).

Addition to notes 461, 463.

461 *Replace "Id.* § 13.4.2.6." *with*: *Id.* § 12.4.2.6.

463 *Replace NCLC UDAP citation with*: National Consumer Law Center, *Unfair and Deceptive Acts and Practices* § 12.6.2 (8th ed. 2012).

Replace notes 464, 466 with:

Page 342

464 *See* National Consumer Law Center, *Unfair and Deceptive Acts and Practices* § 12.8 (8th ed. 2012).

466 National Consumer Law Center, *Unfair and Deceptive Acts and Practices* § 8.8.11 (8th ed. 2012).

9.5 Federal RICO Claims

9.5.1 *Advantages and Disadvantages*

Replace notes 471, 472 with:

471 *See* National Consumer Law Center, Federal Deception Law § 7.7.3 (2012).
472 *Id.* Ch. 7.

Page 343

9.5.2 *Elements of a RICO Claim*

Replace note 478 with:

478 18 U.S.C. § 1961(5); *see* National Consumer Law Center, Federal Deception Law §§ 7.3.3 (pattern of racketeering activity), 7.3.2 (predicate mail fraud and wire fraud offenses) (2012).

Addition to note 481.

481 *Replace NCLC UDAP citation with*: National Consumer Law Center, Federal Deception Law § 7.1.4 (2012).

Replace notes 485–488 with:

485 *See* National Consumer Law Center, Federal Deception Law §§ 7.3.3 (pattern of racketeering activity), 7.3.2 (predicate mail fraud and wire fraud offenses) (2012).
486 *See id.* § 7.4.4.
487 *See id.* § 7.7.2.
488 *See id.* § 7.7.1.

Page 344

Addition to note 489.

489 *Replace NCLC UDAP citation with*: National Consumer Law Center, Federal Deception Law § 7.6.6 (2012).

Replace note 491 with:

491 *See* National Consumer Law Center, Federal Deception Law § 7.8.2 (2012).

9.5.3 *Application to Automobile Fraud Cases*

Replace note 493 with:

493 *See* National Consumer Law Center, Federal Deception Law § 7.3.2 (2012).

Addition to note 500.

500 *Replace NCLC UDAP citation with*: National Consumer Law Center, Federal Deception Law § 7.3.3.3 (2012).

Page 345

Replace notes 504–506 with:

504 *See* National Consumer Law Center, Federal Deception Law § 7.3.3 (2012).
505 *Id.* § 7.4.4.
506 *See id.* § 7.4.6.2.

Addition to note 507.

507 *Replace NCLC UDAP citation with*: National Consumer Law Center, Federal Deception Law § 7.4.6.3 (2012).

9.6 State RICO and Civil Theft Claims

9.6.1 *Overview*

Addition to notes 508, 513.
Page 346

508 *Replace NCLC UDAP citation with*: National Consumer Law Center, Federal Deception Law Appx. F (2012).
513 *Replace NCLC UDAP citation with*: National Consumer Law Center, Federal Deception Law § 8.8 (2012).
 Add: See, e.g., Lykins v. Teta (*In re* Teta), 2011 WL 2435948 (Bankr. D. Colo. June 16, 2011) (dealer's sale of trade-in vehicle without paying off lien is civil theft, and both buyer and previous owner may recover treble damages under civil theft statute); Kesling v. Hubler Nissan, Inc., 975 N.E.2d 367 (Ind. Ct. App. 2012) (fact question whether dealer violated civil theft law by advertising car in misleading way without revealing its serious mechanical problems).

9.6.2 *Advantages of State RICO Claims over UDAP and Federal RICO Claims*

Replace notes 514, 515 with:

514 *See generally* National Consumer Law Center, Federal Deception Law § 8.2.2 (2012).
515 *Id.* § 8.2.1.

Page 347

9.8 Negligence

Addition to note 519.

519 *See, e.g.,* Perry v. Breland, 16 S.W.3d 182 (Tex. App. 2000) (buyer may assert negligence claim against remote seller who signed blank odometer statement in violation of state law).

Chapter 10

Litigating Automobile Fraud Cases

10.3 Pleading and Jurisdiction

10.3.1 Selecting Claims to Plead

Page 352

Replace note 15 with:

15   *See* §§ 8.10, 8.11, *supra. See generally* National Consumer Law Center, Unfair and Deceptive Acts and Practices § 11.6.5 (8th ed. 2012).

Replace sentence containing note 16 with:

The federal odometer statute authorizes $10,000[16] minimum damages or treble damages, whichever is greater.

16   *See* § 6.8.2, *supra.*

Addition to note 17.

17   *Replace NCLC UDAP citation with*: National Consumer Law Center, Unfair and Deceptive Acts and Practices §§ 12.4.1.4, 12.4.2.6, 12.4.3.8 (8th ed. 2012).

Page 353

10.3.2 Drafting the Complaint to Preserve Consumer's Choice of Forum

Replace note 30 with:

30   *See* National Consumer Law Center, Unfair and Deceptive Acts and Practices § 11.5.6 (8th ed. 2012).

10.3.4 Personal Jurisdiction over Out-of-State Defendants

Page 354

10.3.4.1 General Rules

Replace note 45 with:

45   *See* National Consumer Law Center, Unfair and Deceptive Acts and Practices § 11.5.2 (8th ed. 2012) (discussion of long-arm jurisdiction in UDAP cases).

Page 355

Addition to note 53.

53   *Replace Storie v. Duckett Truck Ctr., Inc. citation with*: *See* Storie v. Randy's Auto Sales, L.L.C., 589 F.3d 873 (7th Cir. 2009) (concluding that transferee state's title law applies, not transferor state's title law). *Replace NCLC UDAP citation with*: National Consumer Law Center, Unfair and Deceptive Acts and Practices § 11.5.3 (8th ed. 2012).

Replace note 54 with:

54   *See* National Consumer Law Center, Unfair and Deceptive Acts and Practices § 11.5.3 (8th ed. 2012).

10.3.4.2 Long-Arm Jurisdiction over Out-of-State Vehicle Sellers

Addition to notes 58, 66.

58   *Cf.* Hinners v. Robey, 336 S.W.3d 891 (Ky. 2011) (contracting in Missouri for sale of single vehicle in Kentucky satisfies Kentucky long-arm statute, but exceeds due process limits on jurisdiction).

Page 356

66   *See also* Alisoglu v. Cent. States Thermo King of Okla., Inc., 2012 WL 1666426 (E.D. Mich. May 11, 2012) (Michigan lacks jurisdiction when buyer signed purchase agreement in Oklahoma and accepted delivery there, even though seller communicated with buyer in Michigan and buyer sent payment from Michigan).

Page 357

10.3.4.3 Internet Sales

Addition to notes 67, 71.

67   *Replace Hinners v. Robey citation with*: Hinners v. Robey, 336 S.W.3d 891 (Ky. 2011) (due process does not allow Kentucky jurisdiction over Missouri seller of single vehicle via eBay, when he did not target eBay listing to Kentucky and did not know location of bidders until auction was over). *Replace Riverside Exports, Inc. v. B.R. Crane & Equip., L.L.C. citation with*: 362 S.W.3d 649 (Tex. App. 2011).

71   *Replace Hinners v. Robey citation with*: 336 S.W.3d 891 (Ky. 2011).

10.3.5 Mandatory Arbitration Clauses

Page 358

10.3.5.1 Introduction

Replace note 75 with:

75   (6th ed. 2011 and Supp.).

10.3.5.2 Arbitration Agreement's Existence and Application to the Parties and the Dispute

Replace notes 76, 77, 79, 82 with:

76   National Consumer Law Center, Consumer Arbitration Agreements Ch. 5 (6th ed. 2011 and Supp.).
77   *Id.* § 6.8.4.
79   *Id.* §§ 7.4–7.5.
82   *See* National Consumer Law Center, Consumer Arbitration Agreements § 7.4 (6th ed. 2011 and Supp.).

Page 359

10.3.5.3 If the NAF Is Designated As the Sole Arbitration Forum

Replace notes 85, 86 with:

85   *See* National Consumer Law Center, Consumer Arbitration Agreements § 5.8.1 (6th ed. 2011 and Supp.).
86   *See id.* § 5.8.2.

10.3.5.4 Unconscionability Challenges

Replace notes 89–91 with:

89   (6th ed. 2011 and Supp.).
90   National Consumer Law Center, Consumer Arbitration Agreements § 6.6.3 (6th ed. 2011 and Supp.).
91   *Id.* §§ 4.4, 6.6.4.

Page 360

10.3.5.5 Are Magnuson-Moss Act Claims Subject to Arbitration?

Add to text after sentence containing note 97:

The Ninth Circuit has now reached the same conclusion, although that opinion was later withdrawn.[97.1]

97.1   Kolev v. Euromotors West/The Auto Gallery, 658 F.3d 1024 (9th Cir. 2011), *opinion withdrawn*, 676 F.3d 867 (9th Cir. 2012).

10.3.5.6 Other Grounds to Find an Otherwise Consummated Arbitration Agreement Unenforceable

Replace notes 100–102 with:

100   National Consumer Law Center, Consumer Arbitration Agreements Ch. 8 (6th ed. 2011 and Supp.).
101   *Id.* § 6.8.1.
102   *Id.* § 6.8.2.

Page 361

10.3.5.8 Class Arbitration

Replace notes 106, 107 with:

106   *See* National Consumer Law Center, Consumer Arbitration Agreements § 9.9.2 (6th ed. 2011 and Supp.).
107   *Id.* Ch. 10.

10.3.5.9 Individual Arbitration Seeking Punitive Damages

Replace notes 108, 112, 115 with:

108   *Id.* § 10.7.
112   National Consumer Law Center, Consumer Arbitration Agreements § 10.7.3.4 (6th ed. 2011 and Supp.).
115   National Consumer Law Center, Consumer Arbitration Agreements § 4.4 (6th ed. 2011 and Supp.).

10.4 Liability of Potential Defendants

Page 362

10.4.1 Strategic Considerations

Replace note 118 with:

118   *See* § 10.3.5, *supra*; National Consumer Law Center, Consumer Arbitration Agreements §§ 7.4–7.5 (6th ed. 2011 and Supp.).

10.4.2 Potential Defendants

Replace note 122 with:

122   National Consumer Law Center, Unfair and Deceptive Acts and Practices § 10.3 (8th ed. 2012).

Page 364

10.4.3 Ratification, Acceptance of Benefits, Civil Conspiracy, and Aiding and Abetting

10.4.3.4 Civil Conspiracy

Addition to notes 146, 147.

146   *Replace NCLC UDAP citation with*: National Consumer Law Center, Unfair and Deceptive Acts and Practices § 10.4.2.3 (8th ed. 2012).

147   *Replace NCLC UDAP citation with*: National Consumer Law Center, Unfair and Deceptive Acts and Practices § 10.4.2.3 (8th ed. 2012).

Page 365

10.4.3.5 Aiding and Abetting

Addition to notes 153, 158.

153   *Replace NCLC UDAP citation with*: National Consumer Law Center, Unfair and Deceptive Acts and Practices § 10.4.2.2 (8th ed. 2012).

158   *Replace NCLC UDAP citation with*: National Consumer Law Center, Unfair and Deceptive Acts and Practices § 10.4.2.2 (8th ed. 2012).

Page 366

10.4.4 Recovering from the Creditor for the Dealer's Misconduct

Addition to note 161.

161   *Replace NCLC UDAP citation with*: National Consumer Law Center, Unfair and Deceptive Acts and Practices § 10.5 (8th ed. 2012).

Replace note 162 with:

162   *See* National Consumer Law Center, Unfair and Deceptive Acts and Practices § 10.5 (8th ed. 2012).

Addition to note 165.

165   *Replace NCLC UDAP citation with*: National Consumer Law Center, Unfair and Deceptive Acts and Practices § 10.5.2.4 (8th ed. 2012).

Replace notes 166, 168 with:

166   *See* National Consumer Law Center, Unfair and Deceptive Acts and Practices § 10.5 (8th ed. 2012).

168   National Consumer Law Center, Unfair and Deceptive Acts and Practices § 10.5 (8th ed. 2012).

10.4.5 Liability of Car Auction for Acts of Undisclosed Principal

Addition to note 169.

169   *See also* Castle v. Barrett-Jackson Auction Co., 276 P.3d 540 (Ariz. Ct. App. 2012) (auction company not liable when it repeatedly disclosed that it was not endorsing consignors' descriptions of vehicles; catalog's identification of consignor without including its "d.b.a" is sufficient).

Page 368

10.4.6 On-Line Auctions

Addition to note 182.

182   *Add to Simmons v. Danhauer & Associates, L.L.C. citation: aff'd on other grounds*, __ Fed. Appx. __, 2012 WL 1237795 (4th Cir. Apr. 13, 2012) (S.C. law).

10.5 Discovery

Page 372

10.5.3 Pattern Evidence

Addition to note 225.

225   *See, e.g.*, Kirschenman v. Auto-Owners Ins., 280 F.R.D. 474, 488–491 (D.S.D. 2012) (ordering discovery of other insurance claimants as relevant to punitive damages); *see also* Donovan v. Wal-Mart Stores, Inc., 2012 WL 3025877 (D.S.C. July 24, 2012) (ordering discovery of other incidents involving use of excessive force against suspected shoplifters, as relevant to negligent training claim); Pham v. Wal-Mart Stores, Inc., 2011 WL 5508832 (D. Nev. Nov. 9, 2011) (ordering discovery of other injuries caused by equipment that injured plaintiff store customer, as relevant to whether retailer was on notice of equipment's dangers). *But cf.* Frazier v. Castle Ford, Ltd., 27 A.3d 583, 593–594 (Md. Ct. Spec. App. 2011) (affirming denial of discovery of defendant's past lawsuits and information on all previous extended warranties sold by defendant, including names of purchasers of warranties, when plaintiff had been made whole by extension of the warranty and reimbursement for warranty repairs, and no longer had an interest to act on behalf of the class), *cert. granted*, 33 A.3d 981 (Md. 2011) (table).

10.7 Class Actions

Page 378

10.7.1 In General

Replace "$3000[255]" in sentence containing note 255 with:

$10,000[255]

255   *See* § 6.8.2, *supra.*

Page 379

10.7.2 Shaping the Class Action

Replace "$3000[264]" in sentence containing note 264 with:

$10,000[264]

264   *See* § 6.8.2, *supra.*

Page 380

10.7.3 Claims to Assert in Automobile Fraud Class Actions

Replace note 265 with:

265   *See* National Consumer Law Center, Unfair and Deceptive Acts and Practices § 12.5 (8th ed. 2012); National Consumer Law Center, Federal Deception Law § 7.10 (2012).

Addition to note 269.

269   *Replace NCLC UDAP citation with*: National Consumer Law Center, Unfair and Deceptive Acts and Practices §§ 12.5.4.2.2, 12.5.4.2.9 (8th ed. 2012).

10.7.4 Naming Appropriate Defendants

Addition to note 273.

273   *See* § 10.4.4, *supra*; National Consumer Law Center, Unfair and Deceptive Acts and Practices § 10.5.2.4 (8th ed. 2012).

10.8 Evidentiary Issues

10.8.1 Evidence of Other Bad Acts

Page 382

10.8.1.1 Overview of Admissibility of Other Acts Evidence

Addition to notes 282, 285, 287, 290.

282   *See also* United States v. Turner, 674 F.3d 420, 431 (5th Cir. 2012) (rule applies only to acts "extrinsic to the ones charged"; when evidence of other act and evidence of crime charged are "inextricably intertwined," they are part of a single criminal episode and "other act" evidence is admissible).

285   *See also* United States v. Green, 698 F.3d 48 (1st Cir. 2012) (prior bad acts testimony admissible to explain background of conspiracy).

287   *See also* United States v. Miller, 688 F.3d 322 (7th Cir. 2012) (district court erred by not conducting Rule 403 analysis regarding other bad acts, but error was harmless); United States v. Hsu, 669 F.3d 112, 119 (2d Cir. 2012) (even relevant evidence of other bad acts may be excluded when probative value is substantially outweighed by danger of unfair prejudice); Hendricks v. Ford Motor Co., 2012 WL 4478308, at *3 (E.D. Tex. Sept. 27, 2012) (testimony regarding reasonably similar failures of car jack is admissible to show notice and defect in case alleging manufacturing defect, misrepresentation, and breach of implied warranty).

290   *See also* United States v. Green, 698 F.3d 48 (1st Cir. 2012) (even if other bad acts evidence is admissible under Rule 404(b), it may be excluded if its probative value is substantially outweighed by a danger of unfair prejudice; but not shown here).

Page 384

10.8.1.2 To Show Intent or Motive

Replace note 300 with:

300   *See* National Consumer Law Center, Unfair and Deceptive Acts and Practices §§ 4.2.4, 12.4.2.3.1 (8th ed. 2012).

Addition to note 301.

301   *Replace McCollough v. Johnson, Rodenberg & Lauinger citation with*: 637 F.3d 939 (9th Cir. 2011) (admissible to show malice in malicious prosecution action and intent in Fair Debt Collection Practices Act action).

    Add: See also United States v. Donahue, 460 Fed. Appx. 141 (3d Cir. 2012) (admission of evidence of other bad acts not an abuse of discretion in prosecution for bank fraud, using credit card with intent to defraud, money laundering, and false statements); Guidance Endodontics, L.L.C. v. Dentsply Int'l, Inc., 705 F. Supp. 2d 1265 (D.N.M. 2010) (evidence of prior, similar course of conduct involving unfair trade practices is relevant to willfulness); State v. Conley, 724 S.E.2d 163 (N.C. Ct. App. 2012) (probative value of evidence of other fraudulent check was not outweighed by danger of unfair prejudice in trial for uttering forged instrument and attempting to obtain property by false pretenses).

10.8.1.3 To Show Preparation or Plan

Replace note 305 with:

305 *See* § 10.4.3, *supra*; National Consumer Law Center, Unfair and Deceptive Acts and Practices § 10.3.2 (8th ed. 2012).

10.8.1.4 To Show Knowledge

Addition to notes 307, 308.

307 *See also* Hendricks v. Ford Motor Co., 2012 WL 4478308 (E.D. Tex. Sept. 27, 2012) (testimony regarding similar incidents when car jack failed is admissible to show notice in case alleging manufacturing defect, misrepresentation, and breach of implied warranty); *In re* Porsche Cars N. Am., Inc., __ F. Supp. 2d __, 2012 WL 2953651 (S.D. Ohio July 19, 2012) (claim that manufacturer knew or was reckless in not knowing of alleged defect and that it concealed knowledge from consumers was supported by allegation that manufacturer had received many complaints from owners and lessees regarding the defect at issue).

Page 385

308 *Replace NCLC UDAP citation with*: National Consumer Law Center, Unfair and Deceptive Acts and Practices §§ 10.3, 10.4 (8th ed. 2012).

10.8.1.5 To Show Absence of Mistake or Accident

Addition to note 313.

313 *Replace United States v. Crawford citation with*: 376 Fed. Appx. 185 (3d Cir. 2010).
    Add: See also United States v. Clark, 668 F.3d 568 (8th Cir. 2012) (in identity theft case, prior acts evidence is probative of the defendant's intent, knowledge, and absence of mistake concerning his knowledge that he was using identification of an actual person).

Page 386

10.8.1.6 To Show Habit or Routine Practice

Addition to note 314.

314 *Cf.* Guidance Endodontics, L.L.C. v. Dentsply Int'l, Inc., 705 F. Supp. 2d 1265 (D.N.M. 2010) (conduct must be "reasonably regular and uniform" in order to be deemed a "routine practice"; here, evidence not admissible under Rule 406, but admissible to show defendant's state of mind).

Page 387

10.8.1.8 Admissibility Under RICO and UDAP Statutes

Replace notes 320, 321 with:

320 *See* National Consumer Law Center, Federal Deception Law Chs. 7, 8 (2012).
321 *Id.* § 11.4.3.

Addition to note 322.

322 *See also* Tavenner v. Talon Group, 2012 WL 6022836 (W.D. Wash. Dec. 4, 2012) (stressing percentage of closings in which defendant misstated its third party costs for recording as factor in finding that the alleged conduct affected public interest).

Replace note 323 with:

323 *See* National Consumer Law Center, Unfair and Deceptive Acts and Practices § 2.3.4 (8th ed. 2012).

Page 389

10.8.4 *Evidence of Other Settlements with the Defendant*

Addition to note 344.

344 *But cf.* Armstrong v. HRB Royalty, Inc., 392 F. Supp. 2d 1302 (S.D. Ala. 2005) (Rule 408 excludes evidence of offer to settle a claim only if proffered to prove validity of that claim; evidence of settlement offers in unrelated matters are admissible if relevant).

Page 390

10.8.5 *Parol Evidence Rule and Merger Clauses*

Replace note 353 with:

353 *See* National Consumer Law Center, Unfair and Deceptive Acts and Practices § 4.2.19 (8th ed. 2012).

10.8.6 *Witness Testimony*

Page 396

10.8.6.8 Defendants' Assertion of Fifth Amendment Privilege

Addition to note 406.

406 *Replace Sec. & Exch. Comm'n v. Suman appellate citation with*: 421 Fed. Appx. 86 (2d Cir. 2011).

10.8.7 Documentary Evidence

Page 400

10.8.7.3 Records of Dealer, Manufacturer, Auction House, Repair Shop, and Other Business Entities

Addition to note 438.

438　*See also* Isbell v. Credit Nation Lending Serv., L.L.C., 735 S.E.2d 46 (Ga. Ct. App. 2012) (auction's business records showing that dealer paid for post-sale inspection were admissible even though inspector did not testify).

10.9 Trial of Automobile Fraud Cases

Page 405

10.9.6 Countering Defense Arguments

Replace note 458 with:

458　*See* National Consumer Law Center, Unfair and Deceptive Acts and Practices §§ 4.2.11, 4.3.8, 4.4.1 (8th ed. 2012).

Page 408

10.9.11 Should the Jury Be Told That Actual Damages Will Be Trebled?

Addition to notes 474, 475, 479.
Page 409

474　*Replace Howarth-Tuorney v. Vining citation with*: 162 Wash. App. 1004 (2011).
475　*Replace Howarth-Tuorney v. Vining citation with*: 162 Wash. App. 1004 (2011).
479　*Replace NCLC UDAP citation with*: National Consumer Law Center, Unfair and Deceptive Acts and Practices § 12.4.2.8 (8th ed. 2012).

10.10 Damage Awards

10.10.1 Direct Actual Damages

Page 410

10.10.1.1 Benefit of the Bargain Versus Out-of-Pocket Damages

Replace note 482 with:

482　*See* National Consumer Law Center, Unfair and Deceptive Acts and Practices § 12.1 (8th ed. 2012).

Page 413

10.10.1.4 Introduction of Used Car Guides into Evidence

Addition to notes 520, 523.
Page 414

520　*Replace Dobson v. Saal citation with*: 929 N.Y.S.2d 199 (Civ. Ct. 2011) (table).
523　*Replace In re Herrera citation with*: 454 B.R. 559 (Bankr. E.D.N.Y. 2011).

10.10.2 Cancellation and Recovery of Amount Paid

10.10.2.1 In General

Replace note 528 with:

528　National Consumer Law Center, Unfair and Deceptive Acts and Practices § 12.3.7 (8th ed. 2012).

Page 415

10.10.2.2 Relation to Recovery for Diminished Value

Replace note 533 with:

533　*See* National Consumer Law Center, Unfair and Deceptive Acts and Practices § 12.7.3 (8th ed. 2012).

10.10.3 Incidental and Consequential Damages

10.10.3.1 General

Addition to note 539.

539　*Replace NCLC UDAP citation with*: National Consumer Law Center, Unfair and Deceptive Acts and Practices § 12.3.3 (8th ed. 2012).

Page 417

10.10.3.2 Emotional Distress Damages

Addition to note 549.

549　*Replace NCLC UDAP citation with*: National Consumer Law Center, Unfair and Deceptive Acts and Practices § 12.3.3.9 (8th ed. 2012).

Page 420	### 10.10.5 Statutory Damages

The federal odometer statute provides for $10,000[563] minimum damages.

Replace sentence containing note 563 with:

563   *See* § 6.8.2, *supra.*

Replace note 565 with:

565   *See* National Consumer Law Center, Unfair and Deceptive Acts and Practices § 12.4.1 (8th ed. 2012).

Page 421

10.10.6 Punitive Damages

Addition to note 567.

567   *Replace NCLC UDAP citation with*: National Consumer Law Center, Unfair and Deceptive Acts and Practices § 12.4.1 (8th ed. 2012).

Replace note 568 with:

568   National Consumer Law Center, Federal Deception Law § 7.9.2 (2012).

10.11 Settlement

10.11.1 Settlement Negotiations

10.11.1.6 Dealing with Multiple Defendants and the Dealer's Insurer

Page 425

10.11.1.6.2 Admissibility of evidence of other defendants' settlements; "empty chair" effect

Addition to note 586.

586   *Replace Goodin v. White citation with*: 342 S.W.3d 282 (Ky. Ct. App. 2011).

Page 426

10.11.1.7 Settlements Without Adequate Attorney Fees

Addition to note 594.

594   *Replace NCLC UDAP citation with*: National Consumer Law Center, Unfair and Deceptive Acts and Practices § 12.8.11.3 (8th ed. 2012).

10.12 Attorney Fees in Automobile Fraud Cases

Page 429

10.12.1 Availability of Attorney Fees

Addition to note 608.

608   *Replace NCLC UDAP citation with*: National Consumer Law Center, Unfair and Deceptive Acts and Practices § 12.8 (8th ed. 2012); National Consumer Law Center, Federal Deception Law § 7.9.3 (2012).

10.12.2 Pleading Attorney Fees and Other Initial Steps to Obtain Fees

Addition to note 612.

612   *Replace NCLC UDAP citation with*: National Consumer Law Center, Unfair and Deceptive Acts and Practices § 12.8.7.2 (8th ed. 2012).

10.12.3 Standards for Determining Fees

Replace note 613 with:

613   *See* National Consumer Law Center, Truth in Lending § 11.9 (8th ed. 2012) (discussion of federal decisions on attorney fees).

Addition to note 614.

614   *Replace NCLC UDAP citation with*: National Consumer Law Center, Unfair and Deceptive Acts and Practices § 12.8.11.3.1 (8th ed. 2012).

Page 430

Replace note 615 with:

615   *See* National Consumer Law Center, Unfair and Deceptive Acts and Practices §§ 12.8.11.3.1–12.8.11.3.2 (8th ed. 2012) (discussion of the lodestar formula and the states that use it).

Addition to notes 617, 623.

617   *Replace NCLC UDAP citation with*: National Consumer Law Center, Unfair and Deceptive Acts and Practices §§ 12.8.1, 12.8.11.1 (8th ed. 2012).

623   *Replace NCLC UDAP citation with*: National Consumer Law Center, Unfair and Deceptive Acts and Practices § 12.4.3.8 (8th ed. 2012).

Page 431

10.12.4 Procedure for Requesting Fees

Addition to note 626.

> 626   *Replace NCLC UDAP citation with*: National Consumer Law Center, Unfair and Deceptive Acts and Practices § 12.8.12 (8th ed. 2012).

10.13 Collecting the Judgment

Page 434

10.13.2 Effect of Defendant's Appeal on Collection

Addition to note 641.

> 641   *Replace In re Koksal citation with*: 451 B.R. 144 (Bankr. D. Kan. 2011).

10.13.3 Reaching the Dealer's Insurance Policy

Replace note 645 with:

> 645   National Consumer Law Center, Unfair and Deceptive Acts and Practices § 10.6.2 (8th ed. 2012).

10.13.4 Collecting on a State-Mandated Bond

Page 435

10.13.4.2 What Claimants Does the Dealer's Bond Protect?

Addition to notes 662, 664.

> 662   *But cf.* Brasher's Cascade Auto Auction, Inc. v. Leon, 270 P.3d 330 (Or. Ct. App. 2011) (dealer's "float" agreement with auction is an "inventory finance security agreement" that is excluded from provision of motor vehicle code criminalizing failure to satisfy security interest, so recovery against bond is unavailable).

Page 436

> 664   *But cf.* Brasher's Cascade Auto Auction, Inc. v. Leon, 270 P.3d 330 (Or. Ct. App. 2011) (bond inapplicable to auction's loss caused when dealer obtained titles with insufficient funds checks; dealer's "float" agreement with auction is an "inventory finance security agreement" that is excluded from provision of motor vehicle code criminalizing failure to satisfy security interest, so recovery against bond is unavailable).

Page 439

10.13.4.5 Attorney Fees Collectable Under a Bond

Add to text after sentence containing note 707:

A California decision holds that, when the bond statute was silent about attorney fees, a consumer whose claim against the principal was based on a fee-shifting UDAP statute could collect attorney fees from the surety.[707.1] The court reasoned that the surety's liability is commensurate with that of the principal and thus, because the principal was liable for UDAP attorney fees, the surety was liable also. The fact that the bond covered only fraud was immaterial because the particular UDAP claim at issue amounted to fraud.

> 707.1   Pierce v. Western Sur. Co., 143 Cal. Rptr. 3d 152 (Ct. App. 2012).

Page 440

Addition to note 713.

> 713   *But cf.* Hestead v. CNA Supply, 272 P.3d 547 (Idaho 2012) (statute governing attorney fees in action between insured and insurer does not allow bonding company to recover fees in claimant's unsuccessful suit against it, as claimant is not the insured).

10.13.4.6 Bond Limitations on the Size of a Recovery

Add to text after subsection's third paragraph:

Typically, once the amount of the bond has been paid out to claimants, the surety has no further liability, and additional claimants will receive nothing.[720.1] When the dealer's bond has been exhausted, it is a good idea to investigate the other claims that were paid under the bond. If they were not eligible for payment from the bond,[720.2] the surety may still be liable.

> 720.1   *See, e.g.*, Hestead v. CNA Supply, 272 P.3d 547 (Idaho 2012) (surety that had exhausted the bond by paying several undisputed claims without litigation had no liability to a later claimant, even though that claimant had won a judgment against the dealer).
>
> 720.2   *See* §§ 10.13.4.2, 10.13.4.3, *supra*.

Page 442

10.13.5 Consumer Recovery Funds

Replace note 745 with:

> 745   Andrew v. Cuccinelli, 2010 WL 4906634 (E.D. Va. Dec. 2, 2010), *aff'd*, 445 Fed. Appx. 714 (4th Cir. 2011).

Add to text at end of subsection:

Illinois enacted a dealer recovery fund, effective October 1, 2011, to reimburse retail customers and other dealers who are damaged when a dealer goes out of business without having paid off liens on trade-in vehicles.[755]

In 2011 Ohio created a "title defect rescission fund."[756] The fund, maintained by the attorney general, includes certificate of title fees paid by dealers, certain dealer licensing fees, and certain recoveries and proceeds obtained by the attorney general. In addition, if the attorney general pays a dealer's customer from the fund, that dealer must post a $25,000 bond with the attorney general for the next three years. The fund is available to provide restitution or other remedies to retail purchasers of motor vehicles who suffer damages when a dealer does not have a certificate of title for a used motor vehicle at the time of sale and:

- The dealer fails to obtain a title in the name of the purchaser within forty days;
- The title indicates that the vehicle is a rebuilt salvage or buyback vehicle, and this status was not disclosed to the retail purchaser; or
- The title indicates that the dealer has made an inaccurate odometer disclosure to the buyer.[757]

The statute provides that it is not to be construed as providing for payment of attorney fees to the retail purchaser.[758] At the same time that the legislature created this fund, it repealed a statutory provision that had required all dealers to post a bond during their first three years of licensure.

755   625 Ill. Comp. Stat. § 5/5-102.7.
756   Ohio Rev. Code Ann. §§ 1345.52, 4505.181 (West).
757   Ohio Rev. Code Ann. § 4045.181 (B), (E) (West).
758   Ohio Rev. Code Ann. § 4505.181(K) (West).

Federal Statutes

A.1 The Motor Vehicle Information and Cost Savings Act

A.1.1 Introduction

Delete final "and" from subsection's first paragraph.

Add to text at end of subsection's first paragraph:

and Pub. L. No. 112-141, §§ 31205, 31206, 126 Stat. 760 (2012).

Add to text at end of subsection:

Subsection 32705(g) was added by Pub. L. No. 112-141, § 31205, 126 Stat. 761 (2012).

A.1.2 Text of the Act

§ 32702 Definitions

Add to text after "instrument" in § 32702(5):

or system of components

Add to text at end of § 32702 source citation:

Pub. L. No. 112-141, § 31205, 126 Stat. 760 (2012)

§ 32705 Disclosure requirements on transfer of motor vehicles

Add new subsection to text at end of § 32705:

(g) Electronic disclosures.—Not later than 18 months after the date of enactment of the Motor Vehicle Highway Safety Improvement Act of 2012,[1.1] in carrying out this section, the Secretary shall prescribe regulations permitting any written disclosures or notices and related matters to be provided electronically.

    1.1   *[Editor's note: Enacted July 6, 2012.]*

Add to text at end of § 32705 source citation:

Pub. L. No. 112-141, § 31205, 126 Stat. 761 (2012)

§ 32709 Penalties and enforcement

Replace "$2,000" in § 32709(a)(1) with:

$10,000[1.2]

    1.2   *[Editor's note: Effective October 1, 2012.]*

Replace "$100,000" in § 32709(a)(1) with:

$1,000,000[1.3]

    1.3   *[Editor's note: Effective October 1, 2012.]*

Add source citation at end of § 32709:

[Pub. L. No. 112-141, § 31206, 126 Stat. 761 (2012)]

§ 32710 Civil actions by private persons

Replace "$1,500" in § 32710(a) with:

$10,000[1.4]

    1.4   *[Editor's note: Effective October 1, 2012.]*

Add source citation at end of § 32710:

[Pub. L. No. 112-141, § 31206, 126 Stat. 761 (2012)]

A.1.4 Legislative History

Page 453

*Add new subsection to text
after Appx. A.1.4.9:*

A.1.4.10 2012 Amendments

On July 6, 2012, Congress enacted the Moving Ahead for Progress in the 21st Century Act, Pub. L. No. 112-141, 126 Stat. 405 (2012). This act requires the Department of Transportation to issue regulations by January 6, 2014 which would allow an electronic disclosure or notice to substitute for any written disclosure or notice required by MVICSA. It also makes technical changes to the definition of odometer, increases the amount of minimum statutory damages to $10,000, increases the civil penalties the United States can assess to $10,000, and increases the maximum civil penalty for a related series of violations to $1,000,000. These increases became effective October 1, 2012.

Appendix B Federal Regulations

B.3 National Motor Vehicle Title Information System, 28 C.F.R. §§ 25.51–25.57

Page 491

28 C.F.R. § 25.52 Definitions.

Replace "3102(6)" in definition of Motor vehicle *with:*

30102(6)

Add source citation to text at end of § 25.52:

[77 Fed. Reg. 18,916 (Mar. 29, 2012)]

Page 492

28 C.F.R. § 25.53 Responsibilities of the operator of NMVTIS.

In § 25.53(f)(2) replace "titled" with:

registered

Add source citation to text at end of § 25.53:

[77 Fed. Reg. 18,916 (Mar. 29, 2012)]

State Laws Relating to Automobile Fraud

Replace last sentence of introduction's first paragraph with:

Summaries of each state's UDAP statutes are found in NCLC's *Unfair and Deceptive Acts and Practices* Appx. A (8th ed. 2012). Summaries of each state's RICO statutes are found in NCLC's *Federal Deception Law* Appx. F (2012).

ALABAMA

State Salvage Vehicle Statute: **Ala. Code § 32-8-87**

Replace summary's final sentence with:

Restored salvage title may not be issued for a vehicle of which the frame or a majority of the major component parts were obtained from a junk vehicle. Restored salvage vehicle shall be issued decal, plate, or other emblem to reflect vehicle is rebuilt and which shall be attached to vehicle as described. A vehicle for which an insurer paid a total loss due in part to water damage is deemed a flood vehicle. This must be noted on the certificate of title and disclosed to any purchaser.

ALASKA

Used Car Damage Disclosure: **Alaska Stat. § 45.25.465**

Replace "verify" in summary's first sentence with:

sign

CALIFORNIA

Replace State Salvage Vehicle Statute heading with:

State Salvage Vehicle Statute: **Cal. Veh. Code §§ 544, 5505, 6050, 11515–11515.2, 11713.26 (West)**

Add to text at end of summary:

Before offering a used car for sale, dealers must obtain a vehicle history report which includes information from the National Motor Vehicle Title and Information System and, if the report reveals that the vehicle is a junk or salvage vehicle, or contains a title brand, the dealer must post a warning sticker and provide a copy of the report to the consumer.

GEORGIA

State Salvage Vehicle Statute: **Ga. Code Ann. §§ 40-3-2, 40-3-36, 40-3-37**

Replace "Owner of vehicle" in summary's third sentence with:

Owner of vehicle or trailer

ILLINOIS

State Salvage Vehicle Statute: **625 Ill. Comp. Stat. §§ 5/3-117.1, 5/3-118.1, 5/3-301 to 5/3-308**

Replace "or flood vehicle" in summary's first sentence with:

flood vehicle, or other vehicle

Add to text after summary's first sentence:	Salvage certificate must also be obtained for vehicle that self-insured company determines to be a total loss or that requires repairs exceeding fifty percent of its value.
Replace State Bonding Statute heading with:	**State Bonding Statute: 625 Ill. Comp. Stat. §§ 5/5-101(b)(10), 5/5-102(b)(8), 5/5-102.7** (dealer recovery trust fund)
Add to text at end of Amount *entry:*	In addition, 625 Ill. Comp. Stat. § 5/5-102.7 requires dealers to contribute to a dealer recovery trust fund to reimburse retail customers and other dealers who are damaged when a dealer goes out of business without having paid off liens on trade-in vehicles.

INDIANA

Page 505

Replace State Salvage Vehicle Statute heading with:	**State Salvage Vehicle Statute: Ind. Code §§ 9-22-3-3 to 9-22-3-5, 9-22-3-30, 9-22-3-36**
Add to text before summary's final sentence:	Title for rebuilt vehicle may not designate mileage; it must state "mileage not actual." A vehicle that has been designated junk, dismantled, scrap, or other similar designation in another state shall not be titled in Indiana.
Add to text at end of summary:	Section 9-22-3-36 allows any person aggrieved by a violation of the salvage title laws to bring a civil action for actual damages and attorney fees; court has discretion to treble damages or award $2500, whichever is greater. *See also* Ind. Code § 9-22-3-37 (violation is UDAP violation).
Add to text after State Lemon Laundering Statute summary:	**State Bonding Statute: Ind. Code § 9-23-2-2** *Persons required to post bond*: Any licensee, including automobile auctioneers, dealers, distributors, manufacturers, and wholesale dealers. *Amount*: $25,000. *Persons protected*: State; person aggrieved by violation of Ind. Code ch. 9-23-2 after judgment has been entered. *Scope*: Fines, penalties, costs, and fees owed to state; damages owed pursuant to a judgment in favor of a person aggrieved by a violation of Ind. Code ch. 9-23-2.

LOUISIANA

Page 508

State Salvage Vehicle Statute: La. Rev. Stat. Ann. §§ 32:702, 32:706.1, 32:707, 32:707.3

Add to text at end of summary:	A vehicle with reconstructed title may not be operated as a motor carrier of passengers or a public carrier vehicle. *See also* La. Rev. Stat. Ann. §§ 32:1270.14 (requiring disclosure of flood damage to new or used motorcycles or all terrain vehicles), 32:1270.27 (similar requirement for new or used recreational vehicles).

New Car Damage Disclosure Statute: La. Rev. Stat. Ann. § 32:1264

Add to text at end of summary:	*See also* La. Rev. Stat. Ann. §§ 32:1270.14 (similar damage disclosure requirement for new motorcycles and all terrain vehicles), 32:1270.25 (similar requirement for recreational vehicles).

MINNESOTA

Page 511

State Salvage Vehicle Statute: Minn. Stat. §§ 168A.01, 168A.151, 325F.664 to 325F.6644

Replace summary's first sentence with:	Insurer that acquires ownership of late model vehicle (one with a manufacturer's designated model year equal to or greater than the fifth calendar immediately preceding the current calendar year) or a high value vehicle (one with cash value over $5000 before being damaged, or one over 26,000 lbs. gross vehicle weight that is not a late model vehicle) through payment of damages must apply for salvage certificate.
Replace "70%" in summary's fourth sentence with:	80%

Page 519

OHIO

State Odometer Statute: Ohio Rev. Code Ann. §§ 4549.41 to 4549.99 (West)

Add to text at end of Private civil remedies *entry:*

Ohio Rev. Code Ann. § 4505.181(B) (West) also gives a retail buyer the right to rescind a sale, and to recover from a state fund, if the dealer did not have the certificate of title at the time of sale, and the title indicates that the dealer has made an inaccurate odometer disclosure to the buyer.

Page 520

State Lemon Laundering Statute: Ohio Rev. Code Ann. § 1345.76(A), (B) (West)

Add to text at end of summary:

Ohio Rev. Code Ann. § 4505.181(B) (West) also gives a retail buyer the right to rescind a sale, and to recover from a state fund, if the dealer did not have the certificate of title at the time of sale, and the title indicates that the vehicle is a buyback, and this fact was not disclosed to the buyer in the written purchase agreement.

State Bonding Statute: Ohio Rev. Code Ann. § 4505.181 (West)

Replace entire summary with:

A dealer is required to post a $25,000 bond with the attorney general for three years after the attorney general pays one of the dealer's retail customers from the state motor vehicle recovery fund. The fund is available to provide restitution or other remedies to retail purchasers of motor vehicles who suffer damages when: (1) a dealer does not have a certificate of title for a used motor vehicle at the time of sale; and (2) the dealer either fails to obtain a title in the name of the purchaser within forty days, or the title indicates that the vehicle is a rebuilt salvage or buyback vehicle and this status was not disclosed to the retail purchaser, or the title indicates that the dealer has made an inaccurate odometer disclosure to the buyer.

Page 526

UTAH

State Salvage Vehicle Statute: Utah Code Ann. §§ 41-1a-1001 to 41-1a-1008 (West)

Add to text at end of summary:

A "non-repairable vehicle" is a vehicle with no resale value except as a source of parts or scrap metal (specific standards for vehicle stripped, burned, missing certain parts, and so forth), or that the owner irreversibly designates as a source of parts or for destruction. An insurance company is required to obtain non-repairable title for a non-repairable vehicle. It is unlawful to repair, reconstruct, or restore a non-repairable vehicle.

Page 527

VERMONT

State Lemon Laundering Statute: Vt. Stat. Ann. tit. 9, §§ 4179, 4181

Replace entire summary with:

Any manufacturer or its agent, or any dealer registered in Vermont who attempts to resell a motor vehicle after a final determination, adjudication, or settlement that results in vehicle being returned pursuant to Vermont's or another state's lemon law must apprise prospective buyers in Vermont of this fact in a clearly visible window sticker. Manufacturers, agents, and dealers may not resell in Vermont any vehicle determined or adjudicated as having a serious safety defect. Returned lemon statement must also be conspicuously printed on certificate of title. No liability if seller acquired vehicle without actual knowledge that it was a returned lemon, and title was not branded.

VIRGINIA

State Odometer Statute: Va. Code Ann. § 46.2-112

Add to text at end of Prohibited acts *summary:*

Compliance with 49 U.S.C. § 32704 shall be deemed compliance with Virginia act.

In Civil penalties *summary replace "$1500" with:*

$3000

State Salvage Vehicle Statute: Va. Code Ann. §§ 46.2-1600 to 46.2-1608

Add to text at end of summary:

    A repairable vehicle is a late model vehicle that is neither a rebuilt nor a repaired vehicle, but is repaired to its pre-loss condition by an insurance company and is not accepted by the owner of said vehicle immediately prior to its acquisition by the insurance company as part of the claims process. New Va. Code Ann. § 46.2-1602.2 exempts repairable vehicles from the provisions of the salvage vehicle statute.

State-by-State Information on Requesting Title Histories

As described in Chapter 2, *supra*, obtaining a title history search from a state department of motor vehicles is often a critical step in an automobile fraud investigation. Because of the Driver Privacy Protection Act, applicants must indicate the use they will make of this data and must supply the state with other information. Most states have one or more forms to request a title search available on a state website, other states have forms that are not posted on a website, and some states do not have forms but require a letter or subpoena.

This appendix first sets out for each state the address and website of the state department of motor vehicles. Then it indicates whether a form to request a title search can be found on this treatise's companion website and, if available, an Internet address to check to see if the form on the companion website is still current. If a form is not available, the appendix details other information on the companion website that will assist those seeking to request title searches. This appendix also lists a second address for certain state departments of motor vehicles if that address is a more appropriate one to use to obtain additional information on title searches.

The version of this appendix on this treatise's companion website includes live web links which, if clicked, provide direct access to the relevant state department of motor vehicles website. Finally, there are a number of websites which provide links to the websites of all fifty state departments of motor vehicles. Links to these websites may be found on this treatise's companion website and these links allow rapid access to the various states' websites: www.virtualgumshoe.com/resources/index.asp?CATEGORY_ID=45 and www.pimall.com/nais/dmv.html.

ALABAMA

Alabama Department of Revenue, Motor Vehicle Division, Gordon Persons Building, 50 N. Ripley St., Montgomery, AL 36132 or P.O. Box 327680, Montgomery, AL 36132-7680; www.revenue.alabama.gov. The December 2011 (Form MV-DPPA1) Request for Motor Vehicle Records form to apply for a title search is found on this treatise's companion website, and can also be obtained at www.ador.state.al.us/motorvehicle/mvforms/mvdppa1.pdf or www.revenue.alabama.gov/motorvehicle/forms.cfm. There is a $5 (per vehicle) fee for a printout of the current title record including owner and lienholder information. (Title records are not available for pre-1975 vehicles). There is also a $15 fee (per vehicle) for a complete title history (previous ten years). General information is available from (334) 242-1170.

ALASKA

Alaska Department of Administration, Division of Motor Vehicles, 1300 W. Benson Blvd., Ste. 200, Anchorage, AK 99503-3600; http://doa.alaska.gov/dmv. The October 2009 (Form 851) Request for Research or Verification of Motor Vehicle Record form to apply for a title search is found on this treatise's companion website, and can also be obtained at www.state.ak.us/dmv/forms/pdfs/851.pdf. You must submit a separate form and a $10 fee for each vehicle record for which you are requesting research. General information is available from (907) 269-5551, or (855) 269-5551 (toll free inside Alaska).

ARIZONA

Arizona Department of Transportation, Motor Vehicle Division, P.O. Box 2100, Mail Drop 504M, Phoenix, AZ 85001-2100; www.azdot.gov. The June 2009 (Form 46-4416) Motor Vehicle Record Request form to apply for a title search is found on this treatise's companion website, and can also be obtained at http://mvd.azdot.gov/mvd/FormsandPub/viewPDF.asp?lngProductKey=1281&lngFormInfoKey=1281. There is a $3 (uncertified) and a $5 (certified) fee per record. Some forms must be signed before a notary public or Motor Vehicle Division representative. A customer service guide and drivers license manual with some helpful information on title searches can be found at www.azdot.gov/mvd/custsvcguide.asp. Additional information is available by calling the Motor Vehicle Division at (602) 712-7355 (general inquiries), (602) 255-0072 (Phoenix), (520) 629-9808 (Tucson), or (800) 251-5866 (toll free elsewhere in Arizona). For TDD service call (602) 712-3222 (Phoenix) or (800) 324-5425 (toll free elsewhere in Arizona).

ARKANSAS

Arkansas Department of Finance and Administration, Motor Vehicle Section, Ragland Building, 1900 West Seventh Street, Suite 1100, Little Rock, AR 72201; Department of Finance and Administration, 1509 West 7th Street, Little Rock, AR 72201. Mailing Address: Arkansas Department of Finance and Administration, Attn: Correspondence Desk, P.O. Box 1272, Little Rock, AR 72203; www.state.ar.us/dfa. To qualify to obtain records, first submit a form indicating the requesting party's permissible use. The form will be provided at the Little Rock Motor Vehicle Office. The form and instructions are not available over the Internet, however a copy of the form and instructions to apply for a title search may be found on this treatise's companion website. If you qualify, you may send a written request with a $1 fee for each search plus a $1 fee for each certified copy, or you may establish a search account with the office by sending a deposit of $125. Once your charges deplete the balance to $25, no additional searches will be allowed until payment is made to bring the balance back to $125. Each time you request information by phone $1 will be charged to your account for each search plus $1 for each certified copy requested. If no searches are made during a calendar year period, the search account will be closed and the balance in the account will be remitted to the last address on record. You may open a new account later by completing the Federal Privacy Act forms required for a new account and remitting the $125. If mailing a check to open an account, make check payable to Arkansas Department of Finance and Administration, Motor Vehicle Section, P.O. Box 1272, Little Rock, AR 72203, Attention—Search Accounts. After an account has been established, you may call in with your search request to (501) 682-4692. If mailing a check to request information, make check payable to Arkansas Department of Finance and Administration, Motor Vehicle Section, P.O. Box 1272, Little Rock, AR 72203, Attention—Correspondence Desk. If you do not need copies of documents and only need computer information, you may open an account with the Information Network of Arkansas (INA) at (501) 324-8921 or send an e-mail to info@ark.org.

CALIFORNIA

California Department of Motor Vehicles, Public Operations, Unit-G199, P.O. Box 944247, Sacramento, CA 94244-2470; www.dmv.ca.gov. The December 2011 Instructions for Completing INF 70 Request for Record Information, as well as the December 2011 (Form INF 70) Part I (Record Request) and Part II (Notice to Record Subject) of the Request for Record Information form to apply for a title search, are found on this treatise's companion website, and can also be obtained at www.dmv.ca.gov/forms/inf/inf70.pdf. There is a $5 fee per automated record. There is a $20 fee per year for photocopying of hard copy or microfilm documents. Telephone number for information is (800) 777-0133; for the hearing impaired it is (800) 368-4327 (TTY).

COLORADO

Colorado Department of Revenue, Division of Motor Vehicles, Title Section, 1881 Pierce St., Lakewood, CO 80214; (303) 205-5600; www.colorado.gov/revenue/dmv. The May 2007 (Form DR 2539) Title Information Request and Receipt, the September 2008 (Form DR 2489) Requestor Release and Affidavit of Intended Use, and the March 2010 (Form DR 2539A) Duplicate Title Request and Receipt forms are found on this treatise's companion website, and can also be obtained at www.colorado.gov/cs/Satellite?c=Page&cid=1211879852491& pagename=Revenue-MV%2FRMVLayout. There is a $2.20 per history. Each prior title holder/owner is a separate history. Inquiries by regular mail may be sent to Colorado Department of Revenue, Division of Motor Vehicles, Title Section, Denver, CO 80261-0016. Inquiries by express mail may be sent to Colorado Department of Revenue, Division of Motor Vehicles, Title Section, 1375 Sherman Street, Denver, CO 80203. Walk-in requests may be made at Colorado Department of Revenue, Department of Motor Vehicles, Title Section, 1881 Pierce Street, Denver, CO 80214. Telephone number for titles and registration information is (303) 205-5608; the facsimile number is (303) 205-5978.

CONNECTICUT

State of Connecticut, Department of Motor Vehicles, Copy Record Unit, 60 State St., Wethersfield, CT 06161-0503; www.ct.gov/dmv/site/default.asp. The Title Section may be reached at (860) 263-5710, the Copy Record Unit at (860) 263-5154. The November 2011 (Form J23) Copy Records Request form can be found on this treatise's companion website and can also be obtained at www.ct.gov/dmv/lib/dmv/20/29/j23.pdf. The July 2011 (Form J-23T) Title Copy Records Request form can be found on this treatise's companion website and

can also be obtained at www.ct.gov/dmv/lib/dmv/20/29/j-23t.pdf. Once Form J-23 is submitted, Form J-23T will be mailed to you. You can also request a form by sending an e-mail to dmv.phonecenter@ct.gov, by mailing a request to Department of Motor Vehicles, Phone Center, 60 State St., Wethersfield, CT 06161, or by calling (860) 263-5700 (in the Hartford area or outside of Connecticut) or (800) 842-8222 (toll free within Connecticut only). There is a $20 fee per title history and an additional fee of $20 for certified copy per history. Note: If evidence is needed for tax purposes that ownership of a motor vehicle has been transferred, do not request a Title Search. Instead, request a photocopy of the canceled title. The fee is $20. Certification is an *additional* $20.

DELAWARE

State of Delaware, Division of Motor Vehicles, ATTN: Correspondence, P.O. Box 698, Dover, DE 19903. For overnight delivery, use Federal Express or UPS (not USPS) and send to: DMV, 303 Transportation Circle, Dover, DE 19901; www.dmv.de.gov. The February 2009 (Form MV703) Personal Information Release Form to request a title search is found on this treatise's companion website, and can also be obtained at www.dmv.de.gov/forms/driver_serv_forms/pdfs/personal_rel_form.pdf. The telephone number for questions about vehicle records is (302) 744-2511.

DISTRICT OF COLUMBIA

In order to obtain a title search form from the District of Columbia Department of Motor Vehicles, you must go to one of the three service centers listed: Georgetown Service Center, Georgetown Park Mall-Lower Level, 3222 M Street, N.W., Washington, DC 20007; Penn Branch Service Center, Penn Branch Shopping Center, 3220 Pennsylvania Avenue, S.E., Washington, DC 20019; or Southwest Service Center, 95 M Street, S.W., Washington, DC 20024. There is a $7 fee to obtain a form for title history. The form to request a title search is not available on the DC DMV's website; http://dmv.dc.gov. The telephone number for the service centers is (202) 737-4404. The main telephone number for the District of Columbia Department of Motor Vehicles is (202) 727-5000.

FLORIDA

Florida Department of Highway Safety and Motor Vehicles, Division of Motor Vehicles, 2900 Apalachee Parkway, Mail Stop 73, Neil Kirkman Bldg., Tallahassee, FL 32399-0500; www.hsmv.state.fl.us. The September 2011 (Form HSMV 85054) Motor Vehicle/Vessel Records Request form to request a title search is found on this treatise's companion website, and can also be obtained at www.flhsmv.gov/dmv/forms/BTR/85054.pdf. Fees must accompany this form to avoid a delay in processing your request. For a complete title history a $15 initial payment is required (actual fee calculated at $1 per page). If you have any questions or need additional information, please call the Customer Service Center at (850) 617-2000.

GEORGIA

Georgia Department of Revenue, Motor Vehicle Division, 4125 Welcome All Road, Atlanta, GA 30349; Mailing Address: Georgia Department of Revenue, Motor Vehicle Division, Title Processing—Research, P.O. Box 740381, Atlanta, GA 30374-0381; http://georgia.gov/agencies/georgia-department-revenue-motor-vehicle-division. Telephone: (855) 406-5221; e-mail: motorvehicleinquiry@dor.ga.gov. The July 2011 (Form MV-20) Request for Vehicle Information form to request a title search is found on this treatise's companion website, and can also be obtained at http://motor.etax.dor.ga.gov/forms/pdf/motor/MV_Motor_Vehicle_Data_Request_Form_MV20.pdf. There is a $5 fee per vehicle. More information can be obtained by calling (404) 968-3800 option 7.

HAWAII

Hawaii has county-wide addresses to contact concerning title information. For the County of Honolulu (http://www1.honolulu.gov/csd/vehicle/mvehicle.htm), the address is Department of Motor Vehicle Licensing, City & County of Honolulu, 1041 Nuuanu Ave., 2d Floor, Honolulu, HI 96817, or P.O. Box 30320 or 30330, Honolulu, HI 96820, (808) 532-4325. For the outer islands (Hawaii County) (http://www.hawaiicounty.gov/finance-vrl-general-info): **Hilo Office**—contact Department of Finance, VRL Division, 101 Pauahi St., Suite 5, Hilo, HI 96720, (808) 961-8351; **Kona Office**—contact West Hawaii Civic Center, 74-5044 Ane Keohokalole Highway, Kailua Kona, HI 96740, (808) 323-4818; **Pahoe Office**—contact 15-2615 Keaau-Pahoa Road, Pahoa, HI 96778, (808) 965-2721. For Maui County (http://www.co.maui.hi.us/index.aspx?NID=1328) (islands of Maui, Molokai, Lanai), contact Division of Motor Vehicles and Licensing, 70 E. Kaahumanu Ave., Maui Mall, Suite A-17, Kahului, HI 96732, (808) 270-7363. For Kauai County (http://www.kauai.gov/Government/Departments/Finance/TreasuryDivision/DriversLicense/tabid/169/Default.aspx), contact Island of Kauai, Department of Finance, Treasury Division, Motor Vehicle Department, 4444 Rice St., Bldg. A, Suite 466, Lihue, HI 96766, (808) 241-4256. The state-wide website address is www.co.honolulu.hi.us/main/government. Under state law, title searches can only be conducted in response to a subpoena request. This treatise's companion website contains a sample special proceeding to obtain a subpoena to request a title history in Hawaii.

IDAHO

Idaho Transportation Department, 3311 W. State St., P.O. Box 7129, Boise, ID 83707-1129; (208) 334-8000; https://itd.idaho.gov/dmv/VehicleServices/vs.htm. The September 2012 (Form ITD 3374) Idaho Motor Vehicle Record Request form to request a title search is found on this treatise's companion website, and can also be obtained at http://itD.Idaho.gov/dmv/VehicleServices/documents/3374.pdf. The website now requires the user to log in with a password. There is a $14 fee for each copy of title history obtained. Pay by check or money order made payable to the State of Idaho. Mail to: Titles MVR Desk—Vehicle Services, Idaho Transportation Department, P.O. Box 34, Boise, ID 83731-0034. Information may be obtained by mail from Titles MVR Desk, Idaho Transportation Department, by telephone at (208) 334-8773, or by facsimile at (208) 332-4189.

ILLINOIS

Office of the Secretary of State, Record Inquiry Section, 501 S. Second St., Rm. 408, Springfield, IL 62756-8888; www.illinois.gov and www.cyberdriveillinois.com (Illinois Secretary of State). The September 2010 (Form VSD 375.15) Information Request Form to request a title search can be found on this treatise's companion website, and can also be obtained at www.cyberdriveillinois.com/publications/pdf_publications/vsd375.pdf. There is a fee of $5 for each title search. The telephone number to obtain more information is (217) 785-3000; the facsimile number is (217) 524-0122.

INDIANA

Indiana Bureau of Motor Vehicles, Indiana Government Center North, Room N405, Vehicle Records Section, 100 North Senate Ave., Indianapolis, IN 46204; http://indiana.gov/bmv. The August 2011 (State Form 46449) Request for Motor Vehicle or Watercraft Records form to request a title search is found on this treatise's companion website, and can also be obtained at www.in.gov/bmv/2344.htm (scroll down to the Driver or Vehicle Records Request section and click on the link to this form). There is an $8 fee for each title history. More information can be obtained by calling (317) 233-6000.

IOWA

Iowa Motor Vehicle Division, 6310 S.E. Convenience Blvd., Ankeny, IA 50021; Mailing Address: Office of Vehicle Services, Iowa Department of Transportation, Motor Vehicle Division, P.O. Box 9278, Des Moines, IA 50306-9278; www.dot.state.ia.us/mvd/index.htm. The January 2009 (Form 431069) Privacy Act Agreement for Request of Motor Vehicle Records form to request a title search is found on this treatise's companion website, and can also be found at https://forms.iowadot.gov/FormsMgt/External/431069.pdf. The telephone numbers to obtain more information are (800) 532-1121 (toll-free in Iowa), (515) 244-9124 or (515) 244-8725; the facsimile number is (515) 237-3056.

KANSAS

Kansas Department of Revenue, Titles and Registration, 915 S.W. Harrison, Topeka, KS 66626-0001; www.ksrevenue.org/vehicle.html. The July 2011 (Form TR/DL 302) Motor Vehicle Records form to request a title search is found on this treatise's companion website, and can also be obtained at www.ksrevenue.org/pdf/trdl302.pdf. There is a fee to obtain title history. The telephone number for more information is (785) 296-3621.

KENTUCKY

Transportation Cabinet, Division of Motor Vehicle Licensing, P.O. Box 2014, Frankfort, KY 40622-2014, Attn: Records Management; www.kytc.state.ky.us. The February 2009 (Form TC 96-16) Request for Motor Vehicle Record Which Includes Personal Information form to request a title search is found on this treatise's companion website, and can also be obtained at http://mvl.ky.gov/MVLWeb/pdf/TC96-016.pdf. A $2 fee (check or money order made payable to Kentucky State Treasurer) is required with the completed form, fees are subject to change. For more information call (502) 564-2737; the facsimile number is (502) 564-1686.

LOUISIANA

Louisiana Department of Public Safety and Corrections, Public Safety Services, Office of Motor Vehicles, P.O. Box 64886, Baton Rouge, LA 70896 (mailing address); the street address is 7979 Independence Blvd., Baton Rouge, LA 70806 (physical location); http://omv.dps.state.la.us. The form to request a title search is found on this treatise's companion website, and can also be obtained at http://dpsweb.dps.louisiana.gov/DPSForms.nsf (select form category "Governmental Agency Request," then choose the "Credential or Vehicle Information Request" form). The telephone number for more information is (225) 925-6146.

MAINE

Bureau of Motor Vehicles, Title Section, 29 State House Station, 101 Hospital St., Augusta, ME 04333-0029 (physical location); www.state.me.us/sos/bmv. Please call (207) 624-9000 ext. 52138 and ask representative to mail you an Affirmation Statement package which you have to sign in order to obtain a title history; or call (877) 456-8195 (TTY for the hearing impaired); or send request by facsimile to (207) 624-9254. A copy of the Affirmation Statement is found on this treatise's companion website.

MARYLAND

Title Files, Motor Vehicle Administration, 6601 Ritchie Hwy. NE, Glen Burnie, MD 21062, www.MVA.Maryland.gov. The November 2012 (Form DR-057) Request for Motor Vehicle Administration Records form to request a title search is found on this treatise's companion website, and can also be obtained at http://mva.state.md.us/Resources/DR-057.pdf. For more information call (410) 768-7000 or (800) 950-1682 (to speak with a customer service representative), and (800) 492-4575 (TTY for the hearing impaired).

MASSACHUSETTS

Massachusetts Department of Transportation, Registry of Motor Vehicles (RMV), P.O. Box 55889, Boston, MA 02205-5889; www.state.ma.us/rmv. There are two forms to complete in order to obtain a title history search, the July 2012 (Form T21078-0310) Request for Personal Information in RMV Records form, found at www.massdot.state.ma.us/Portals/16/docs/21078.pdf, and the October 2011 (Form 21087-1109) Title History Search or Photocopy form, found at www.mass.gov/rmv/forms/21087.pdf. These forms are also found on this treatise's companion website, and can both be obtained at www.mass.gov/rmv/titles/7search.htm. Mail the completed forms and a check with the appropriate fee(s), payable to MassDOT, to: Massachusetts Registry of Motor Vehicles, Title Division, P.O. Box 55885, Boston, MA 02205-55885; Attn.: Court Records (for certified records only) or Attn.: Mail Listings (for all other requests). If you have any questions, call the Title Division at (857) 368-8050. For help call the customer assistance bureau at (617) 351-9580. The telephone numbers for more information are (617) 351-4500 (if you are calling from area codes 339, 617, 781, or 857, or from out-of-state), (800) 858-3926 (if you are calling from area codes 351, 413, 508, 774, or 978), and (877) 768-8833 (if you are calling from Massachusetts and are hearing impaired).

MICHIGAN

Michigan Department of State, Record Lookup Unit, 7064 Crowner Drive, Lansing, MI 48918-1540; www.michigan.gov/sos. The Michigan Department of State has two forms to request a title search—both are found on this treatise's companion website. The September 2010 (Form BDVR-153) Requesting Your Own Record form is for those who are requesting a title history for a vehicle they own. This form can also be obtained at www.michigan.gov/documents/bdvr153_16280_7.pdf. The September 2010 (Form BDVR-154) Record Lookup Request form is for those who are requesting a title history for a vehicle that does not belong to them. This form can also be obtained at www.michigan.gov/documents/bdvr154_16269_7.pdf. Requests for records can be made by mail, by phone (must have an account), or by facsimile (must have an account or pay with a credit card). To use the mail option, complete the BDVR 153 or 154 form in detail, meeting one of the thirteen permissible reasons if requesting a record other than your own vehicle's. Each record is $7 and may be charged to your Discover, Visa or Mastercard, or include a check or money order made payable to the State of Michigan. For help completing this form call (517) 322-1624. Completed requests may be sent by facsimile to (517) 322-1181 and must be charged to a credit card.

MINNESOTA

Minnesota Department of Public Safety, Driver and Vehicle Services, Records Unit, 445 Minnesota St., Suite 161, St. Paul, MN 55101-5161; www.dps.state.mn.us/dvs. The April 2012 (Form PS2502A-18) DVS Records Request form to request a title search is found on this treatise's companion website, and can also be obtained at https://dps.mn.gov/divisions/dvs/forms-documents/Documents/RecordRequestForm.pdf. There is a fee for record request: $1 per printed page, in addition to the record or certified recopy copy fee. Please refer to form. The telephone number for the unit is (651) 215-1335 or (651) 282-6555 (TTY); the facsimile number is (651) 282-5512.

MISSISSIPPI

Mississippi Department of Revenue, Motor Vehicle Licensing Bureau, P.O. Box 1140, Jackson, MS 39215 (mailing address); the street address is 1577 Springridge Road, Raymond, MS 39154 (physical location); www.dor.ms.gov. The nine-page (Form 77969) package (available at www.dor.ms.gov/docs/mvl_disclosurepacket.pdf), consisting of the NOTICE To All Persons Requesting Information From Motor Vehicle Records (one page), the February 2012 (Form 77-601-12-1-1-000) Request for Motor Vehicle Records Information (five pages), the February 2012 (Form 77-600-12-1-1-000 Motor Vehicle Records Disclosure Form (one page), the February 2012 (Form 77-600-12-1-2-000) Reason(s) the Motor Vehicle Record Will Be Used (one page), and the Motor Vehicle Licensing Bureau and Title Bureau Fees (one page) forms, is found on this treatise's companion website, and can also be obtained at www.dor.ms.gov/title/title_forms.html. The telephone number for the Motor Vehicle Licensing Bureau is (601) 923-7100 and its facsimile number is (601) 923-7133; the Title Bureau's facsimile number is (601) 923-7224.

MISSOURI

Missouri Department of Revenue, Motor Vehicle Bureau, 301 West High St., Room 370, Jefferson City, MO 65101; http://dor.mo.gov/mvdl/motorv. Missouri has a two-step process. The first step is to complete Form 4678, relating to the requester's qualifications under the Driver's Privacy Protection Act. The November 2012 (Form 4678) Request for Security Access Code form is found on this treatise's companion website, and can also be obtained at http://dor.mo.gov/forms/4678.pdf. Then one submits an application for a particular vehicle's records. This July 2009 (Form 4803) Request for Information form is found on this treatise's companion website, and can also be obtained at http://dor.mo.gov/forms/4803.pdf. One can also request Form 4678 by calling (573) 751-4300, and Form 4803 by calling (573) 526-3669, or by visiting http://dor.mo.gov/mvdl/motorv/forms. One can also set up an account so that one can send requests by facsimile and be billed monthly, by calling (573) 526-7367 and requesting the appropriate forms. An example of a facsimile request used by a Missouri consumer attorney is found on this treatise's companion website. Contact Motor Vehicle Bureau at (573) 526-3669.

MONTANA

Montana Department of Justice, Motor Vehicle Division, Title and Registration Bureau, 1003 Buckskin Drive, Deer Lodge, MT 59722-2375; https://doj.mt.gov/driving. The October 2012 (Form MV210) Release of Motor Vehicle Records form to request a title search is found on this treatise's companion website, and can also be obtained at https://doj.mt.gov/wp-content/uploads/MV210.pdf and www.doj.mt.gov/driving/forms/mv210.pdf. Refer to form for proper fee(s) and form of payment. The telephone number for the division is (406) 444-3661; the facsimile number is (406) 846-6039; or you can send an e-mail to mvdtitleinfo@mt.gov.

NEBRASKA

Nebraska Department of Motor Vehicles, Driver and Vehicle Records Division, 301 Centennial Mall South, P.O. Box 94789, Lincoln, NE 68509-4789; www.dmv.state.ne.us. The August 2008 Application for Copy of Vehicle Record form to request title searches is found on this treatise's companion website, and can also be obtained at www.dmv.state.ne.us/dvr/pdf/vehrecapp.pdf. Refer to form for proper fee(s) and payment. Make checks payable to the Department of Motor Vehicles. A stamped self-addressed envelope is required for all mail-in requests. The telephone number for the department is (402) 471-3918.

NEVADA

Nevada Department of Motor Vehicles, Central Services Records Section, Department of Motor Vehicles, 555 Wright Way, Carson City, NV 89711-0250; http://www.dmvnv.com. The seven-page packet, consisting of the October 2009 (Form IR006) Individual Package Instructions (one page), the January 2012 (Form IR002) Application for Record Information (one page), the May 2012 (Form IR003) Affidavit (one page), the September 2008 (Form IR015) Letter of Authorization to Release Information (one page), and the May 2012 (Form IR005) Guidelines and Fees for Record Inquiries (three pages) forms, is found on this treatise's companion website, and can also be obtained at www.dmvnv.com/pdfforms/ir002.pdf. The telephone number for the department is (775) 684-4590.

NEW HAMPSHIRE

New Hampshire Department of Safety, Division of Motor Vehicles, 23 Hazen Drive, Concord, NH 03305; www.nh.gov/safety/divisions/dmv. The September 2012 (Form DSMV 505) Release of Motor Vehicle Records form to request a title search is found on this treatise's companion website, and can also be obtained at www.nh.gov/safety/divisions/dmv/forms/documents/dsmv505.pdf. Refer to form for proper fee(s) and payment. The telephone number for title information is (603) 227-4150; the facsimile number is (603) 271-1061.

NEW JERSEY

New Jersey Motor Vehicle Commission, Certified Information Unit, P.O. Box 146, Trenton, NJ 08666-0146; www.state.nj.us/mvc. The August 2010 (Form DO-22A) Title Search form to request title searches is found on this treatise's companion website, and can be obtained at www.state.nj.us/mvc/pdf/Vehicles/DO-22a.pdf and also at www.state.nj.us/mvc/Vehicle/Copies.htm. To request a certified photocopy of a title (current owner information only): (1) complete and sign the Request for Title Search (Form DO-22A) and include the make, year, vehicle identification number, and detailed reason for

request; (2) submit a photocopy of your driver's license; and (3) submit a $15 check or money order made in payable to NJMVC. Mail required documents to: NJ Motor Vehicle Commission, Certified Information Unit, 225 East State St., P.O. Box 146, Trenton, NJ 08666-0146. Note: Both pages one and two must be completed and submitted for the request to be considered. A separate request is required for each vehicle. For questions about completing the forms call the Certified Information Unit at (609) 292-4102.

NEW MEXICO

State of New Mexico, Taxation and Revenue Department, Motor Vehicle Division, Joseph Montoya Building, P.O. Box 1028, 1100 South St. Francis Drive, Santa Fe, NM 87504-1028; www.mvd.newmexico.gov/Pages/Home.aspx. The March 2001 (MVD-11260) Confidential Records Release form to request title searches is found on this treatise's companion website, and can also be obtained at www.mvd.newmexico.gov/SiteCollectionDocuments/assets/mvd11260.pdf. The telephone number for title information is (888) 683-4636.

NEW YORK

New York State Department of Motor Vehicles, 6 Empire State Plaza, Albany, NY 12228; www.dmv.ny.gov. The December 2010 (MV-15) Instructions for Requesting DMV Record Information Using Form MV-15 (four pages) form to request a title search is found on this treatise's companion website, and can also be obtained at www.dmv.ny.gov/forms/mv15.pdf. There is a $10 fee for vehicle title record. Make your check or money order (exact fee, no starter checks accepted) payable to the Commissioner of Motor Vehicle, MV-15 Processing, NYS Department of Motor Vehicles, 6 Empire State Plaza, Albany, NY 12228. The telephone number for the Title Service Bureau is (518) 486-4714.

NORTH CAROLINA

North Carolina Division of Motor Vehicles, 1100 New Bern Ave., Raleigh, NC 27697; www.ncdot.gov/DMV. The January 2008 (MVR-605A) Request for Motor Vehicle Information form to request title searches is found on this treatise's companion website, and can also be obtained at www.ncdot.gov/download/dmv/VR_MVR605A.pdf. Refer to form for fee application and mailing. The telephone number for the division is (919) 715-7000.

NORTH DAKOTA

North Dakota Department of Transportation, Motor Vehicle Division, 608 East Blvd. Avenue, Bismarck, ND 58505-0780; www.dot.nd.gov. The July 2010 (SFN 51269) Request for Vehicle Information form to request title searches is found on this treatise's companion website, and can also be obtained at www.dot.nd.gov/forms/sfn51269.pdf. Fee is $3 per vehicle or $3 per search if none found. The telephone number for the division is (701) 328-2725; the facsimile number is (701) 328-1487.

OHIO

Ohio Department of Public Safety, Bureau of Motor Vehicles, P.O. Box 16520, Columbus, OH 43216-6520 (mailing address); the street address is 1970 West Broad Street, Columbus, OH 43223-1101 (physical location); www.bmv.ohio.gov or www.ohiobmv.com. The July 2012 (BMV 1173) OBMV Record Request form to request title searches is found on this treatise's companion website, and can also be obtained at http://publicsafety.ohio.gov/links/bmv1173.pdf. Certain basic information is available on-line at the department's website. A more complicated process is required to obtain copies of the actual titles, because each county stores titles issued in that county. To begin your inquiry at www.bmv.ohio.gov or www.ohiobmv.com, click the link for Vehicle Title Inquiry under the section entitled "BMV Online Services" and enter the vehicle identification number (VIN) or title number. A "hot print" provides a list of titles issued on that vehicle in Ohio. The county issuing each title is identified by the first two numbers of the title number, and "quick links" at www.bmv.ohio.gov or www.ohiobmv.com list the codes for each county. Then request title information from the relevant counties, using the form found on this treatise's companion website, which can also be obtained at http://publicsafety.ohio.gov/links/bmv1173.pdf. There is a $5 fee to obtain a copy of title record. It is possible to request the complete title jacket, which may include repossession affidavits, auction receipts, or other useful documentation. Make check or money order payable to Ohio Treasurer Josh Mandel. Mail the completed form to: Ohio Bureau of Motor Vehicles, Attention: Record Request, P.O. Box 16520, Columbus, OH 43216-6520. Results will be mailed to requestor. Note: An additional $3.50 fee will be charged when submitting this form in person to the Customer Service Center located at 1970 W. Broad St., Columbus, OH 43223. The telephone number for the Bureau of Motor Vehicles is (614) 752-7500.

OKLAHOMA

Oklahoma Tax Commission, Motor Vehicle Division, 2501 N. Lincoln Blvd., Oklahoma City, OK 73194; www.oktax.state.ok.us. The January 2013 (Form 769) Vehicle Information Request form to request title searches is found on this treatise's companion website, and can also be obtained at www.tax.ok.gov/mvforms/769.pdf. There is a $7.50 fee for a microfilm title history and a $10 fee for a certified title history. The fee is due regardless of whether any documents are located. The telephone number for the division is (800) 522-8165, option 5, ext. 1-3120, toll free for in-state calls; the direct telephone number is (405) 521-3120, ext. 139 or 143.

OREGON

Oregon Department of Transportation, Drivers and Motor Vehicles Services, 1905 Lana Ave., N.E., Salem, OR 97314-2250; www.oregon.gov/ODOT. The June 2012 (735-7122) Request for Information form to request title searches is found on this treatise's companion website, and can also be obtained at www.odot.state.or.us/forms/dmv/7122.pdf. There is a $22.50 fee for vehicle title history. Send the completed form, required documentation, and fee (check or money order payable to Oregon DMV) to: DMV Record Services, 1905 Lana Avenue, N.E., Salem, OR 97314-2250. The telephone number for the department is (888) 275-6368; the facsimile number is (503) 986-3432.

PENNSYLVANIA

Pennsylvania Department of Transportation, Bureau of Driver Licensing, Vehicle Record Services, P.O. Box 68691, Harrisburg, PA 17106-8691; www.dmv.state.pa.us. The September 2010 Request for Vehicle Information form to request title searches is found on this treatise's companion website, and can also be obtained at www.dmv.state.pa.us/pdotforms/dl_forms/dl-135.pdf. There is a $5 fee for each record request or a $10 fee for each certified record. Send completed form(s) along with your check or money order to the address listed above. The telephone numbers for more information are (800) 932-4600 (in-state), (717) 412-5300 (out-of-state), (800) 228-0676 (TDD in-state), or (717) 412-5380 (TDD out-of-state).

RHODE ISLAND

State of Rhode Island, Division of Motor Vehicles, 600 New London Avenue, Cranston, RI 02920-3024; www.dmv.ri.gov. The August 2010 Request for Title Information form to request a title search is found on this treatise's companion website, and can also be obtained at www.dmv.ri.gov/documents/forms/title/Request_Title_Information.pdf. There is a $51.50 fee per vehicle identification number (VIN). For more information call the division's main number at (401) 462-4368; or the title section at (401) 462-5774.

SOUTH CAROLINA

South Carolina Department of Public Safety, 10311 Wilson Blvd., Blythewood, SC 29016; Mailing Address: P.O. Box 1993, Blythewood, SC 29016; www.scdps.gov. The June 2010 (5027-A) Request for Vehicle Information form to apply for a title search is found on this treatise's companion website, and can also be obtained at www.scdmvonline.com/DMVNew/forms/5027-A.pdf. There is a $6 fee for title history. For records to be processed within 72 hours, please include an additional $20 (expedite fee) for each record. Cash is not accepted. Make checks payable to the SC Department of Motor Vehicles and mail to: Titles Mail-In Unit, P.O. Box 1498, Blythewood, SC 29016-0024. The telephone number for the DMV Call Center is (803) 896-5000. For general requirements for DMV Services, please call the 24-hour customer service line at (800) 442-1368. In Columbia, please call 896-8623.

SOUTH DAKOTA

South Dakota Department of Revenue, Division of Motor Vehicles, Records Search Section, 445 E. Capitol Ave., Pierre, SD 57501-3185; http://dor.sd.gov. The November 2008 (MV/DPPA) Driver's Privacy and Protection Act form to request a title search is found on this treatise's companion website, and can also be obtained at www.state.sd.us/eforms/secure/eforms/nonE0821V4-DriversPrivacyAndProtectionAct.pdf. There is a $5 fee for copies of paperwork on microfilm for title history. Note: The form must be signed, dated, notarized, and accompanied by the appropriate fee before your request will be processed. Completed forms should be sent to address listed above. The telephone number for the division is (605) 773-3541.

TENNESSEE

Tennessee Department of Revenue, Vehicle Services Division, 500 Deaderick Street, Andrew Jackson Building, Nashville, TN 37242; www.tennessee.gov/revenue. The June 2012 (RV-F1313801) Vehicle Information Request form to request title searches is found on this treatise's companion website, and can also be obtained at www.tennessee.gov/revenue/forms/titlereg/f1313801Fill-in.pdf. There is a $15 fee per title history. Mail completed forms and payment to: State of Tennessee, Department of Revenue, Vehicle Services Division, 44 Vantage Way, Suite 160, Nashville, TN 37243-8050. The division's telephone number is (615) 253-0600.

TEXAS

Department of Transportation, Vehicle Titles and Registration Division, 125 E. 11th St., Austin, TX 78701-2483 (mailing address); the street address is 4000 Jackson Ave., Austin, TX 78731 (physical location); www.txdmv.gov. The September 2011 (VTR-275) Request for Texas Motor Vehicle Information form to request a title search is found on this treatise's companion website, and can also be obtained at www.txdot.gov/txdoteforms/GetForm?formName=/VTR-275.xdp&appID=/VTR&status=/reportError.jsp&configFile=WFServletConfig.xml. There is a fee of $5.75 for a title history and a fee of $6.75 for a certified title history. Send check, money order, or cashier's check made payable to TxDMV. Do not mail cash. Submit completed and signed form with copy of your government issued photo identification (and written authorization, if applicable) to: TxDMV, Vehicle Titles and Registration Division, Austin, TX 78779-0001, or visit a TxDMV Regional Office for assistance. The division's telephone number is (512) 465-7611 (outside Austin); (512) 837-4416 (in Austin); the facsimile number is (512) 302-2162.

UTAH

Utah State Tax Commission, Motor Vehicle Division, P.O. Box 30412, Salt Lake City, UT 84130 (for express services (FedEx, UPS, etc.), use zip code 84116); http://dmv.utah.gov. The April 2011 (TC-890) Release of Protected Motor Vehicle Information form to request title searches is found on this treatise's companion website, and can also be obtained at http://tax.utah.gov/forms/current/tc-890.pdf. The telephone number for the division is (801) 297-7780 (Salt Lake City area); (800) 368-8824 (toll-free), or send an e-mail to dmv@utah.gov.

VERMONT

State of Vermont, Department of Motor Vehicles, 120 State St., Montpelier, VT 05603-0001; www.dmv.vermont.gov. The May 2012 (TA-VG-116) Vermont DMV Record Request form to request title searches is found on this treatise's companion website, and can also be obtained at http://dmv.vermont.gov/sites/dmv/files/pdf/DMV-VG116-Record_Request.pdf. Refer to application form for applicable fees. The telephone number for the department is (802) 828-2000; for TTD please call (800) 253-0191; the facsimile number is (802) 828-2098; or you may also send an e-mail to CommissionersOffice@state.vt.us.

VIRGINIA

Virginia Department of Motor Vehicles, P.O. Box 27412, Richmond, VA 23269-0001; www.dmv.state.va.us. The April 2002 (CRD 01) Request for Vehicle Information by a Prospective Purchaser form to request a title search is found on this treatise's companion website, and can be obtained at www.dmv.state.va.us/webdoc/pdf/crd01.pdf. The department's telephone number is (804) 497-7100 or (866) 368-5463.

WASHINGTON

Washington State Department of Licensing, Public Disclosure, P.O. Box 2957, Olympia, WA 98507-2957; www.dol.wa.gov. The July 2011 (RPD-224-003) Vehicle/Vessel Information Disclosure Request form to request title searches is found on this treatise's companion website, and can also be obtained at www.dol.wa.gov/forms/224003.pdf or www.dol.wa.gov/forms/formstitle.html#t (click on the link "Vehicle/Vessel Information Disclosure Request"). The department's facsimile number is (360) 570-7088. Please mail your request to the address above or send your completed forms by facsimile, or send an e-mail to vsdisclose@dol.wa.gov.

WEST VIRGINIA

West Virginia Department of Transportation, Division of Motor Vehicles, P.O. Box 17150, Charleston, WV 25317; www.transportation.wv.gov/Pages/default.aspx. The May 2011 (DMV 100) Request for Vehicle Information Form to request title searches is found on this treatise's companion website, and can also be obtained at www.transportation.wv.gov/dmv/Forms/DMVForms/DMV-100-TR_Request-for-Information.pdf. There is a $25 fee for title history. The division's telephone number is (304) 926-3909; the facsimile number is (304) 926-3881.

WISCONSIN

Vehicle Records Section, Wisconsin Department of Transportation, P.O. Box 7911, Madison, WI 53707-7911; www.dot.wisconsin.gov/drivers/index.htm. The January 2010 (MV2896) Vehicle/Driver Record Information Request form to request a title search is found on this treatise's companion website, and also at www.dot.wisconsin.gov/drivers/forms/mv2896.pdf. There is a $5 fee for each non-certified motor vehicle record and a $10 fee for each certified motor vehicle record. You may reach the section at (414) 266-1000 or (608) 261-2583.

WYOMING

Wyoming Department of Transportation, Motor Vehicle Services, 5300 Bishop Blvd., Cheyenne, Wyoming 82009-3340; www.dot.state.wy.us/wydot. The January 2010 Vehicle Record and Privacy Disclosure Release form to request title searches is found on this treatise's companion website, and can also be obtained at www.dot.state.wy.us/wydot/titles_plates_registration/title_search and click on the "Vehicle Record and Privacy Disclosure Release" link at the bottom of the page or go to www.dot.state.wy.us/files/content/sites/wydot/files/shared/Motor%20Vehicle%20Services/PRIVACY%20DISCLOSURE%20RELEASE.pdf. All requests for searches should be directed in writing to the address above. There is a $5 fee for a motor vehicle record. The telephone number for headquarters is (307) 777-4375; the facsimile number is (307) 777-4772; or titles and registration may be reached at (307) 777-4825 or (307) 777-4851.

Sample Documents

Page 546

*Add new subsection to text
after Appx. E.2:*

E.3 Sample Reports Which Include Data from the National Motor Vehicle Title and Information System

This appendix reprints two sample reports from different providers which include data from the National Motor Vehicle Title and Information System (NMVTIS). A full-color version of the reports may be found on this treatise's companion website. Although NMVTIS is a government database, reports are not available directly from the government. Instead, reports must be purchased from an approved provider. A list of current providers may be found at www.vehiclehistory.gov. Prices range from $2.00 to $34.99, depending on the provider and the type of report. For more information about the NMVTIS database see § 2.3.4, *supra*.

NMVTIS VEHICLE HISTORY REPORT

VIN 5FACP45202S783210
YEAR 2010 MAKE FORD

A "Brand" defines the status of a vehicle, such as Theft, Flood, Salvage or Rebuilt. A brand is carried with the title as the vehicle travels from state to state. There are over 250 brands recognized by NMVTIS that can be categorized by type.

BRAND CATEGORY	NMVTIS SEARCH RESULT
Total Loss	No Brand Reported
Salvage	No Brand Reported
Disclosed Damage	No Brand Reported
Bond	No Brand Reported
Flood	Brand Found: **Salt Water Damage**

Applied By: New Jersey   **Applied On:** 11/02/2012

Brand Explanation: This vehicle has been damaged in a salt water flood.

CARS/Cash for Clunkers	No Brand Reported
Gray Market	No Brand Reported
Junk	No Brand Reported
Manufacturer Brand	No Brand Reported
New/Re-Issued VIN	No Brand Reported
Odometer	No Brand Reported
Rebuilt/Repaired/Reconstructed	Brand Found: **Rebuilt**

Applied By: Missouri   **Applied On:** 03/20/2013

Brand Explanation:
The vehicle, previously branded "salvage", has passed anti-theft and safety inspections, or other jurisdiction procedures, to ensure the vehicle was rebuilt to required standards. Also known as prior salvage (salvaged).

1

Dismantled	No Brand Reported
Rental/Taxi/Police	No Brand Reported
Agricultural/Logging Vehicle	No Brand Reported
Title Copy	No Brand Reported
Antique/Classic	No Brand Reported
Undisclosed Lien	No Brand Reported

Current Title Information

State	VIN	Issue Date	Odometer
Missouri	5FACP45202S783210	05/06/2013	000045843 Miles

Historical Title Information

State	VIN	Issue Date	Odometer
New Jersey	5FACP45202S783210	10/17/2010	000000014 Miles
New Jersey	5FACP45202S783210	11/02/2012	000045208 Miles

If you need more information, please contact the State of Missouri at http://dor.mo.gov/mvdl/motorv/.

If you are a business and need more information, please contact the State of New Jersey by visiting http://www.state.nj.us/mvcbiz/Records/index.htm .
If you are an individual and need more information, please contact the State of New Jersey by visiting http://www.state.nj.us/mvc/ .

2

Reporting Occurrence	Reporting Entity Information	Date Obtained	Vehicle Intended for Export?	Vehicle Disposition
1	INSURANCE SALVAGE AUCTIONS, INC ALBANY, NY Phone: 5556478952	12/29/2012	NO	**NOT REPORTED** At the time of this reporting the vehicle disposition was not known.
2	INSURANCE SALVAGE AUCTIONS, INC ALBANY, NY Phone: 5556478952	12/29/2012	NO	**SOLD** This vehicle has been sold.

Reporting Occurrence	Reporting Entity Information	Date of Total Loss Declaration or Date Total Loss Claim Paid
1	INSURANCE DIRECT, INC CHAMPLAIN, IL Phone: 5558675309 Email: CLAIMS@INSDIRECT.COM	10/31/2012

Lien Count   There is 1 lien reported for this vehicle.

Lien data does not include information on all motor vehicles in the United States because not all lien holders provide lien information to ADD's data provider.

DETAILED VEHICLE INFORMATION

Standard Data

Body Type	2D Convertible	**Manufactured**	United States
Drive Line	Rear Wheel	**Engine Type**	4.0L V6 EFI
Fuel Type	Gas	**Make**	Ford
Model	Mustang	**Corporation**	Ford
Model Year	2005	**Production Seq. No.**	211633
Trim Level	Base	**Vehicle Class**	2D Convertible

Interior

Seats - Passenger	2-way adjuster, manual	**Seats - Rear**	Split-bench
Floor Mats	Carpet	**Storage**	Glovebox, lockable
Clock	Included	**Air Conditioning**	Manual
Power Locks	Door	**Visors**	Mirror
Seats - Driver	4-way adjuster, manual	**Power Outlet(s)**	12-volt, 2
Audio - CD/MP3	CD	**Consoles**	Storage
Seats	Fold flat	**Seats - Front**	Buckets
Armrests	Full length	**Windows**	Power
Remote Releases	Deck lid	**Carpet**	Included
Audio - Radio	AM/FM	**Cargo Area**	Carpet
Theft Deterrent Systems	SecuriLock	**Steering Column**	Tilt

Mechanical

Exhaust	Stainless steel muffler & tailpipe	**Steering**	Power; Rack & pinion
Cruise Control	Included	**Brakes - Rear**	Disc, vented
Brake Calipers - Front	2-piston; Aluminum; Floating	**Brake Calipers - Rear**	Floating; Iron; Single piston
Brakes - Front	Disc, vented		

Safety

Safety Belt Systems	Belt Minder	**Airbag - Front Passenger**	2nd Generation
Child Seat Anchors	LATCH	**Remote Keyless Entry**	Included
Airbag - Driver	2nd Generation	**Crash Sensors**	Fuel Shutoff Switch
3-Pt Seat Blts - All Pos	Included		

Suspension

Stabilizer Bar	Front	**Struts**	MacPherson, front
Springs	Coil, rear		

Warranty

Bumper-to-Bumper	3-year/36,000-mile

NOTE: Detailed Vehicle Information is obtained by decoding the Vehicle Identification Number (VIN). The equipment currently installed in the vehicle may differ from the equipment listed in the report (i.e. the possibility exists that the vehicle may have been modified or rebuilt).

5

NMVTIS CONSUMER ACCESS PRODUCT DISCLAIMER

NMVTIS Consumer Access Product Disclaimer

The National Motor Vehicle Title Information System (NMVTIS) is an electronic system that contains information on certain automobiles titled in the United States. NMVTIS is intended to serve as a reliable source of title and brand history for automobiles, but it does not contain detailed information regarding a vehicle's repair history.

All states, insurance companies, and junk and salvage yards are required by federal law to regularly report information to NMVTIS. However, NMVTIS does not contain information on all motor vehicles in the United States because some states are not yet providing their vehicle data to the system. Currently, the data provided to NMVTIS by states is provided in a variety of time frames; while some states report and update NMVTIS data in "real-time" (as title transactions occur), other states send updates less frequently, such as once every 24 hours or within a period of days.

Information on previous, significant vehicle damage may not be included in the system if the vehicle was never determined by an insurance company (or other appropriate entity) to be a "total loss" or branded by a state titling agency. Conversely, an insurance carrier may be required to report a "total loss" even if the vehicle's titling-state has not determined the vehicle to be "salvage" or "junk."

A vehicle history report is NOT a substitute for an independent vehicle inspection. Before making a decision to purchase a vehicle, consumers are **strongly encouraged to also obtain an independent vehicle inspection** to ensure the vehicle does not have hidden damage. The Approved NMVTIS Data Providers (look for the NMVTIS logo) can include vehicle condition data from sources other than NMVTIS.

NMVTIS data **INCLUDES** (as available by those entities required to report to the System):

- Information from participating state motor vehicle titling agencies.
- Information on automobiles, buses, trucks, motorcycles, recreational vehicles, motor homes, and tractors. NMVTIS may not currently include commercial vehicles if those vehicles are not included in a state's primary database for title records (in some states, those vehicles are managed by a separate state agency), although these records may be added at a later time.
- Information on "brands" applied to vehicles provided by participating state motor vehicle titling agencies. Brand types and definitions vary by state, but may provide useful information about the condition or prior use of the vehicle.
- Most recent odometer reading in the state's title record.
- Information from insurance companies, and auto recyclers, including junk and salvage yards, that is required by law to be reported to the system, beginning March 31, 2009. This information will include if the vehicle was determined to be a "total loss" by an insurance carrier.
- Information from junk and salvage yards receiving a "cash for clunker" vehicle traded-in under the Consumer Assistance to Recycle and Save Act of 2009 (CARS) Program.

Consumers are advised to visit http://www.vehiclehistory.gov/ for details on how to interpret the information in the system and understand the meaning of various labels applied to vehicles by the participating state motor vehicle titling agencies.

ADD Consumer Access Disclaimer

Auto Data Direct, Inc. is a "read-only portal" of data stored in the NMVTIS databases. Data is passed directly from AAMVA to the client through the ADD interface, which has been tested and approved by AAMVA. ADD does not enter the information found on a NMVTIS record, nor is it responsible for the accuracy or verification of the information found therein. The motor vehicle records accessed by ADD clients are recorded by participating states and are current with those entities at the time of access through the ADD portal.

6

instaVIN Vehicle History & Title Report

Record Summary
2007 Chevrolet Impala
VIN 2G1WB58K579351034

Body: **Sedan**

Engine Displacement: **4 Li**

Drive Train Type: **FWD**

Run Date: **05/01/13 09:43 am PDT**

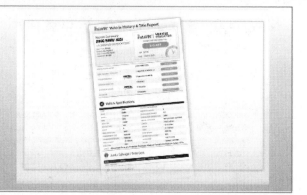

Vehicle Specification		2007 Chevrolet Impala
Junk/Salvage/Total Loss		2 reported incidents
Title Information	NMVTIS	5 events
Odometer		3 events
Other Information		0 events

✳ Vehicle Specifications

Year	2007	Engine Displacement	4 Li
Make	Chevrolet	Engine Aspiration	N/A
Model	Impala	Fuel Capacity	17
Trim	LS	Fuel Type	F
Body Type	Sedan	Length	200
Vehicle Type	Car	Height	59
Doors	4	Width	73
Drive Train Type	FWD	Curb Weight	3555
Transmission Type	A	Gross Vehicle Weight	0
Plant	OSHAWA #1: ONTARIO, CANADA	Wheelbase	111
Engine Configuration	V6		
Safety	DRIVER AND PASSENGER FRONT, FRONT AND REAR HEAD AIRBAGS, ACTIVE BELTS, AND OCCUPANT SENSOR		

⛔ Junk / Salvage / Total Loss

Date	Entity	Disposition	Intended for Export	Damage Type	Data Source
04/12/13	NEW JERSEY			Brand: Salvage	NMVTIS

2007 Chevrolet Impala VIN 2G1WB58K579351034 -- 05/01/13 09:43 am PDT -- Page 1/8

instaVIN Vehicle History & Title Report

 ## Junk / Salvage / Total Loss

Date	Entity	Disposition	Intended for Export	Damage Type	Data Source
02/12/13	Fairfield, CA Copart, Inc. Phone: 7076395294		No	(Junk And Salvage,)	NMVTIS

Current Title Information

Date	State of Title	Mileage	Event

This information reflects the current Title information on file with NMVTIS. For more information, please contact the state of Title below.

Date	State of Title	Mileage	Event
04/12/13	New jersey	93,002	Title and Registration

 ## Additional Title Information

Date	State of Title	Mileage	Event

This information includes historical Title information associated with this vehicle on file with NMVTIS. Historical Title data may vary from state to state and may not include all Title records from the in-service date. For more information, please contact the state(s) of Title below.

Date	State of Title	Mileage	Event
04/12/13	New jersey		Brand: Salvage
04/12/13	New jersey		Brand: Not Actual Odometer
10/22/10	New jersey	93,001	Title and Registration
10/14/10	New jersey	92,853	Title and Registration

 ## Title Brand Information

⊗ Salvage	✓ No Former Rental
✓ No Junk	✓ No Police Vehicle
✓ No Cash for Clunkers	✓ No Taxi Vehicle
✓ No Total Loss	✓ No Street Rod
✓ No Disclosed Damage	✓ No Antique
✓ No Flood Damage	✓ No Classic
✓ No Fire Damage	✓ No Logging Vehicle
✓ No Hail Damage	✓ No Agricultural Vehicle
✓ No Undisclosed Lien	✓ No Kit Assembly
✓ No Prior Non-Repairable/Repaired	✓ No Test Vehicle
✓ No Vandalism	✓ No Replica

insta**VIN** Vehicle History & Title Report

Title Brand Information

⊘ No Collision	⊘ No Gray Market
⊘ No Dismantled	⊘ No Manufacturer's Buy-Back
⊘ No Refurbished	⊘ No Title Facsimile Document
⊘ No Rebuilt	⊘ No Reissued VIN
⊘ No Reconstructed	⊘ No Owner Retained Salvage
⊘ No Crushed	⊘ No Prior Owner Retained
⊘ No Remanufactured	⊘ No Vehicle Non-Conformity
⊘ No Warranty Return	⊘ No Recovered Theft
⊘ No Vehicle Safety Defect	⊘ No Bond Posted
⊘ No VIN Replaced by a New State Assigned VIN	

ADDITIONAL ODOMETER BRAND INFORMATION

⊘ Odometer Does Not Exceed Mechanical Limits	⊘ No Odometer Discrepancy
⊗ Odometer May Be Altered	⊘ Not Exempt from Odometer Disclosure
⊘ No Odometer Replacement	⊘ No Other Odometer Problem Exists

 Odometer

Date	Mileage	Problems Reported	Data Source
04/12/13	93,002	N/A	NMVTIS
10/22/10	93,001	N/A	NMVTIS
10/14/10	92,853	N/A	NMVTIS

 Other Information

Date	Event	Location	Other Information
		No other information reported to instaVIN.™	

🏛 Legal Disclaimer

CONSUMER ACCESS PRODUCT DISCLAIMER

2007 Chevrolet Impala VIN 2G1WB58K579351034 -- 05/01/13 09:43 am PDT -- Page 3/8

ı̃nstaVIN Vehicle History & Title Report

The National Motor Vehicle Title Information System (NMVTIS) is an electronic system that contains information on certain automobiles titled in the United States. NMVTIS is intended to serve as a reliable source of title and brand history for automobiles, but it does not contain detailed information regarding a vehicle's repair history.

All states, insurance companies, and junk and salvage yards are required by federal law to regularly report information to NMVTIS. However, NMVTIS does not contain information on <u>all</u> motor vehicles in the United States because some states are not yet providing their vehicle data to the system. Currently, the data provided to NMVTIS by states is provided in a variety of time frames; while some states report and update NMVTIS data in real-time (as title transactions occur), other states send updates less frequently, such as once every 24 hours or within a period of days.

Information on previous, significant vehicle damage may not be included in the system if the vehicle was never determined by an insurance company (or other appropriate entity) to be a "total loss" or branded by a state titling agency. Conversely, an insurance carrier may be required to report a "total loss" even if the vehicle's titling-state has not determined the vehicle to be "salvage" or "junk."

The information in this system **INCLUDES:**
- Information from participating state motor vehicle agencies.
  - Information on automobiles, buses, trucks, motorcycles, recreational vehicles, motor homes, and tractors. NMVTIS may not currently include commercial vehicles if those vehicles are not included in a state's primary database for title records (in some states, those vehicles are managed by a separate state agency), although these records may be added at a later time.
- Information on "brands" applied to vehicles provided by participating state motor vehicle titling agencies. Brand types and definitions vary by state, but may provide useful information about the condition or prior use of the vehicle.
  - Most recent odometer reading in the state's title record.
- Information from insurance companies, and auto recyclers, including junk and salvage yards, that is required by law to be reported to the system, beginning March 31, 2009. This information will include if the vehicle was determined to be a "total loss" by an insurance carrier.
  - Information from junk and salvage yards receiving a "cash for clunker" vehicle traded-in under the Consumer Assistance to Recycle and Save Act of 2009 (CARS) Program.

Consumers are advised to visit www.vehiclehistory.gov for details on how to interpret the information in the system and understand the meaning of various labels applied to vehicles by the participating state motor vehicle titling agencies.

instaVIN™ CONSUMER ACCESS DISCLAIMER

The compilation of instaVIN™ vehicle history reports requires data from multiple third party data suppliers and other various data sources which may supplement data supplied by NMVTIS or its sources. Sections of this Vehicle History Report indicated with an asterisk (*) are based on NMVTIS data and NMVTIS data sources. Thus, the above Consumer Access Product Disclaimer applies solely to NMVTIS data and NMVTIS data sources. NMVTIS provides data directly from its databases to instaVIN™ consumers through the AAMVA tested and approved instaVIN™ interface on a "read-only" basis. instaVIN™ does not supply or enter any data into the NMVTIS databases and is not responsible for supplying any data contained in any NMVTIS Vehicle History Report. Therefore, instaVIN™ cannot warrant or guarantee the accuracy of any information contained in any NMVTIS Vehicle History Report data.

In the event that NMVTIS Vehicle History Report Data shows current and historical states of title, as provided in any NMVITIS Vehicle History Report, instaVIN™ consumers have several options regarding full vehicle history records from the current and historical states of title. These records, if such records exist, are available for purchase. Please contact customerservice@instavin.com. Should you require more information, please contact the state of current title and the state of historical title as provided on your Report. This information is subject to change from time to time and is accessible here: http://instavin.com/AAMVAStateList.html

instaVIN Vehicle History & Title Report

NMVTIS Brand Definition Glossary

Brand Name	Description
Flood damage	Vehicle damaged by freshwater flood (or it is unknown whether the damage was caused by fresh water or saltwater).
Fire damage	Vehicle damaged by fire.
Hail damage	Vehicle damaged by hail.
Saltwater damage	Vehicle damaged by saltwater flood.
Vandalism	Vehicle damaged by vandals.
Kit	A Vehicle that has been built by combining a chassis with a different (non-matching VIN) frame, engine, and body parts. The VIN on the chassis is used as the vehicle's VIN.
Dismantled	The vehicle can only be sold as parts and can not be legally driven.
Junk	The vehicle is incapable of safe operation for use on the roads or highways and has no resale value except as a source of parts or scrap, or the vehicle's owner has irreversibly designated the vehicle as a source of parts or scrap. This vehicle shall never be titled or registered. Also known as non-repairable, scrapped, or destroyed.
Rebuilt	The vehicle, previously branded "salvage", has passed anti-theft and safety inspections, or other jurisdiction procedures, to ensure the vehicle was rebuilt to required standards. Also known as prior salvage (salvaged).
Reconstructed	A vehicle that has been permanently altered from original construction by removing, adding, or substituting major components.
Salvage--Damage or Not Specified	Any vehicle which has been wrecked, destroyed or damaged, to the extent that the total estimated or actual cost of parts and labor to rebuild or reconstruct the vehicle to its pre-accident condition and for legal operation on roads or highways exceeds a jurisdiction-defined percentage of the retail value of the vehicle. The retail value of the vehicle is determined by a current edition of a nationally recognized compilation (to include automated data bases) of retail values. Salvage--Damage or Not Specified also includes any vehicle to which an insurance company acquires owner- ship pursuant to a damage settlement, or any vehicle that the vehicle's owner may wish to designate as a salvage vehicle by obtaining a salvage title, without regard to extent of the vehicle's damage and repairs, or any vehicle for which the jurisdiction cannot distinguish the reason the vehicle was designated salvage.
Test Vehicle	The vehicle is built and retained by the manufacturer for testing.
Refurbished	Any vehicle modified by the installation of a new cab and chassis for the existing coach which has been renovated, resulting in a vehicle of greater value or a vehicle with a new style.
Collision	Vehicle damaged by collision.
Salvage Retention	The vehicle is branded salvage and is kept by the owner.
Prior Taxi	Vehicle previously registered as a taxi.
Prior Police	Vehicle previously registered as a police vehicle.
Original Taxi	Vehicle is currently registered as a taxi.
Original Police	Vehicle is currently registered as a police vehicle.
Remanufactured	Vehicle was reconstructed by the manufacturer.
Warranty Return	Vehicle returned to the manufacturer because of a breach in the warranty.
Antique	The vehicle is over 50 years old.

instaVIN Vehicle History & Title Report

Classic	The vehicle is over 20 years old and adheres to other jurisdiction-specific criteria, e.g., vehicle make, condition, etc.
Agricultural Vehicle	The vehicle will primarily be operated on private roads for agricultural purposes.
Logging Vehicle	The vehicle will primarily be operated on private roads for logging purposes.
Street Rod	The vehicle has been modified to not conform with the manufacturer's specifications, and the modifications adhere to jurisdiction-specific criteria.
Vehicle Contains Reissued VIN	The chassis VIN has been reissued, i.e. the same VIN is reused.
Replica	A vehicle with a body built to resemble and be a reproduction of another vehicle of a given year and given manufacturer.
Totaled	A vehicle that is declared a total loss by a jurisdiction or an insurer that is obligated to cover the loss or that the insurer takes possession of or title to.
Owner Retained	A vehicle that has been declared by the insurance company to be a total loss but the owner maintains possession and ownership of the vehicle.
Bond Posted	The insurance company has issued a bond on the vehicle because the ownership of the vehicle cannot be proven; this allows the vehicle to be sold and titled. Note: This brand is not valid after January 17, 2003.
Memorandum Copy	The title document is a facsimile title and not the active (original or duplicate) title document.
Recovered Theft	The vehicle was previously titled as salvage due to theft. The Vehicle has been repaired and inspected (or complied with other jurisdiction procedures) and may be legally driven.
Undisclosed Lien	The vehicle has entered the titling jurisdiction from a jurisdiction that does not disclose lien-holder information on the title. The titling jurisdiction may issue a new title without this brand if no notice of a security interest in the vehicle is received, within a jurisdiction-defined timeframe. Note: This brand is not valid after January 17, 2003.
Prior Owner	A vehicle that was previously branded owner retained and Retained was sold. The new owner's title contains this brand.
Vehicle Non- conformity Uncorrected	A non-safety defect reported to the jurisdiction by the vehicle manufacturer remains uncorrected.
Vehicle Non- conformity Corrected	A non-safety defect reported to the jurisdiction by the vehicle manufacturer has been corrected.
Vehicle Safety Defect Uncorrected	A safety defect reported to the jurisdiction by the vehicle manufacturer remains uncorrected.
Vehicle Safety Defect Corrected	A safety defect reported to title jurisdiction by the vehicle manufacturer has been corrected.
VIN replaced by a new state assigned VIN	A title should not be issued for the VIN. This brand can be issued for rebuilt vehicles.
Gray Market	Vehicle was manufactured for use outside the United States and has been brought into the United States. The vehicle is not in compliance with applicable federal standards. OR: Vehicle was manufactured for use outside the United States and has been brought into the United States. The vehicle is in compliance with applicable federal standards.
Manufacturer Buy Back	A vehicle that has been bought back by the manufacturer under jurisdiction -defined regulations or laws, such as lemon laws. For example, the manufacturer could be obligated to buy back the vehicle when a specified number of repair attempts fail to correct a major problem on a new vehicle, or if a new vehicle has been out of service for repair for the same problem for a cumulative period of 30 days or more, within one year of purchase.

instaVIN Vehicle History & Title Report

Former Rental	Former Rental
Salvage--Stolen	Any vehicle the reporting jurisdiction considers salvage because an insurance company has acquired ownership pursuant to a settlement based on the theft of the vehicle.
Salvage--Reasons Other Than Damage or Stolen	Any vehicle the reporting jurisdiction considers salvage based on criteria, such as abandonment, not covered by the Salvage-- Damage or Not Specified and Salvage-Stolen Brands. Note--Percent of damage is not reported with brand.
Disclosed Damage	The vehicle has sustained damage to the extent that the damage is required to be disclosed under the jurisdiction's damage disclosure law.
Prior Non Repairable I Repaired	A vehicle constructed by repairing a vehicle that has been destroyed or declared to be non-repairable or otherwise declared to not be eligible for titling because of the extent of damage to the vehicle but has been issued a title pursuant to state law after falling within this criterion with this brand on th e face of the certificate of title.
Crushed	The frame or chassis of the vehicle has been crushed or otherwise destroyed so that it is physically impossible to use it in constructing a vehicle.

ODOMETER BRANDS

Actual	The true mileage for the vehicle. The odometer has not been tampered with, reached its mechanical limits, or been altered.
Not Actual	The odometer reading is known to be other than the true mileage for the vehicle. OR: Odometer tampering verified--the odometer reading is known to be other that the true mileage for the vehicle, due to tampering.
Exempt from Odometer Disclosure	The vehicle falls within criteria that allow it to change ownership without disclosure of the odometer reading.
Exceeds Mechanical Limits	The odometer reading is less than the true mileage of the vehicle because the odometer cannot display the total number of true miles.
Odometer may be Altered	The titling authority has reason to believe that the odometer reading does not reflect the true mileage of the vehicle because of an alteration to the odometer.
Odometer Replaced	The odometer in the vehicle is not the odometer put in the vehicle when manufactured.
Reading at Time of Renewal	The odometer reading was recorded when the registration was renewed.
Odometer Discrepancy	The titling authority has reason to believe that the odometer reading does not reflect the true mileage of the vehicle because of known previous recorded values of odometer for the vehicle.
Call Title Division	The titling authority knows of some problem with the odometer reading that it cannot print on a title. Titling authority will discuss the problem (manual process) with authorized inquirers.
Rectify Previous Exceeds Mechanical Limits Brand	A state other than the brander corrected Exceeds Mechanical Limit.
Pending Junk Automobile - CARS.gov	The National Highway Traffic Safety Administration - (NHTSA) Consumer Assistance to Recycle and Save (CARS) program is processing an application, which, if approved, will render this vehicle incapable of operating on public streets, roads, and highways. The vehicle will have no value except as a source of parts or scrap, shall be crushed or shredded within a specified time period (including the engine block), and shall not be exported prior to crushing or shredding. For additional information concerning the CARS program visit CARS.gov.

2007 Chevrolet Impala VIN 2G1WB58K579351034 -- 05/01/13 09:43 am PDT -- Page 7/8

ȋnstaVIN Vehicle History & Title Report

Junk Automobile -CARS.gov	Pursuant to the Consumer Assistance to Recycle and Save Act of 2009 (CARS) this vehicle is incapable of operating on public streets, roads, and highways. The vehicle has no value except as a source of parts or scrap, shall be crushed or shredded within a specified time period (including the engine block), and shall not be exported prior to crushing or shredding. For additional information concerning the CARS program visit CARS.gov.

OTHER EVENTS

Lien	Vehicle has a reported open lien or outstanding loan through a lender or lenders.
Listed for Sale	Vehicle reported for current or historical sale online.
Towing/Impound	Vehicle has been reported to have been towed or impounded.
Export	Vehicle has been reported as exported.
Active Theft	Vehicle is reported to be an active theft in either the US, Canada or Mexico. Check with local law enforcement.
Recovered Theft	Vehicle is reported to have been previously stolen in either the US, Canada or Mexico and later recovered.
Total Loss	Vehicle has been reported to be a Total Loss vehicle by an insurance company.

2007 Chevrolet Impala VIN 2G1WB58K579351034 -- 05/01/13 09:43 am PDT -- Page 8/8

Appendix F State Automobile Dealer Licensing Offices

replacement appendix

ALABAMA

Alabama Department of Revenue
Motor Vehicle Division
Dealer Licenses
P.O. Box 327643
Montgomery, AL 36132-7643
Phone: (334) 242-9000 Fax: (334) 353-8835

ALASKA

Alaska Department of Administration
Division of Motor Vehicles
Attn: Dealer/Fleet
1300 W. Benson Blvd., Suite 300
Anchorage, AK 99503-3691
Phone: (907) 269-3755 Fax: (907) 269-3762

ARIZONA

Arizona Department of Transportation
Motor Vehicle Division
Dealer Licensing Unit, Mail Drop 552M
P.O. Box 2100
Phoenix, AZ 85001-2100
1801 W. Jefferson St.
Phoenix, AZ 85007
Phone: (602) 255-0072 Fax: (602) 712-3268

ARKANSAS

Arkansas State Police
Vehicle Dealers License Administrator
Attn: Used Motor Vehicles
No. 1 State Police Plaza Drive
Little Rock, AR 72209
Phone: (501) 618-8606 or (501) 618-8617
Fax: (501) 618-8587

CALIFORNIA

California Department of Motor Vehicles
Occupational Licensing Unit
P.O. Box 932342
Sacramento, CA 94232-3420
Phone: (916) 229-3126 Fax: (916) 229-4728

COLORADO

Overnight Mailing Address:
Colorado Department of Revenue
Auto Industry Licensing Division
1881 Pierce St., #112
Lakewood, CO 80214

Regular Mailing Address:
Colorado Department of Revenue

Auto Industry Licensing Division
Denver, CO 80261-0016
Phone: (303) 205-5604 Fax: (303) 205-5977

CONNECTICUT

Connecticut Department of Motor Vehicles
Dealers and Repairers Division
60 State St.
Wethersfield, CT 06161
Phone: (860) 263-5056 Fax: (860) 263-5554

DELAWARE

Delaware Motor Vehicle Division
Dealer Information
Rte. 113, 303 Transportation Circle
P.O. Box 698
Dover, DE 19903
Phone: (302) 744-2503 or (302) 744-2500
Fax: (302) 739-2602

DISTRICT OF COLUMBIA

Department of Consumer & Regulatory Affairs
Business Services Division
1100 4th Street, S.W., Room 4600 East
Washington, DC 20024
Phone: (202) 442-4311 or (202) 442-4400
Fax: (202) 442-9445

FLORIDA

Florida Division of Motor Vehicles
Dealer Licensing Section, MS 65
Neil Kirkman Building, Room A312
2900 Apalachee Parkway
Tallahassee, FL 32399-0630
Phone: (850) 617-3003 Fax: (850) 617-5217

GEORGIA

Georgia Secretary of State
Professional Licensing Boards Division
Used Motor Vehicle Dealers and Parts Dealers
237 Coliseum Dr.
Macon, GA 31217-3858
Phone: (478) 207-2440 Fax: (877) 588-0446

HAWAII

Department of Commerce & Consumer Affairs
Professional & Vocational Licensing Division
Attn: MVI
P.O. Box 3469

Honolulu, HI 96801
Phone: (808) 586-3000 Fax: (808) 586-3031

IDAHO

Idaho Transportation Department
Division of Motor Vehicles
Vehicle Services Section
3311 W. State Street (Zip Code: 83703)
P.O. Box 7129
Boise, ID 83707-1129
Phone: (208) 334-8681

ILLINOIS

Illinois Secretary of State
Vehicle Services Department
Dealer Licensing Section
Howlett Building
501 S. Second St., Room 069
Springfield, IL 62756
Phone: (217) 782-7817 Fax: (217) 524-0120

INDIANA

Secretary of State
Auto Dealer Services Division
302 W. Washington Street, Room E-018
Indianapolis, IN 46204
Phone: (317) 234-7190 Fax: (317) 233-1915

IOWA

Iowa Department of Transportation
Office of Vehicle Services
P.O. Box 9278
Des Moines, IA 50306-9278
Phone: (515) 237-3110 Fax: (515) 237-3056

KANSAS

Kansas Department of Revenue
Division of Motor Vehicles
Dealer Licensing
Docking State Office Building
915 S.W. Harrison St.
Topeka, KS 66626-0001
Phone: (785) 296-3621 Fax: (785) 296-3852

KENTUCKY

Kentucky Motor Vehicle Commission
105 Sea Hero Rd., Suite 1
Frankfort, KY 40601
Phone: (502) 573-1000 Fax: (502) 573-1003

LOUISIANA

Used Motor Vehicle Commission
3132 Valley Creek Dr.
Baton Rouge, LA 70808
Phone: (225) 925-3870 Fax: (225) 925-3869

Louisiana Motor Vehicle Commission
3519 12th St.
Metairie, LA 70002
Phone: (504) 838-5207 Fax: (504) 838-5416

MAINE

Maine Department of State
Bureau of Motor Vehicle
Dealer and Agent Services
101 Hospital St.
State House Station #29
Augusta, ME 04333
Phone: (207) 624-9000 ext. 52143 Fax: (207) 624-9037

MARYLAND

Maryland Vehicle Administration
Business Licensing and Consumer Services
6601 Ritchie Highway N.E.
Glen Burnie, MD 21062
Phone: (410) 768-7000

MASSACHUSETTS

Contact city or town where the business is located.

MICHIGAN

Michigan Department of State
Business Licensing and Regulation Division
Licensing Unit
430 W. Allegan
Lansing, MI 48918
Phone: (888) 767-6424 Fax: (517) 335-2810

MINNESOTA

Department of Public Safety
Drivers and Vehicle Services, Dealers Unit
445 Minnesota Street, Suite 186
St. Paul, MN 55101-5155
Phone: (651) 215-1328 Fax: (651) 297-1480

MISSISSIPPI

Mississippi State Tax Commission
Motor Vehicle Licensing Bureau
1577 Springridge Rd.
Raymond, MS 39154-9602

Mailing Address:
P.O. Box 1140
Jackson, MS 39215-1140
Phone: (601) 923-7000 Fax: (601) 923-7133

MISSOURI

Missouri Department of Revenue
Motor Vehicle Bureau
Dealer Licensing Section
301 West High Street, Room 370
P.O. Box 43
Jefferson City, MO 65105
Phone: (573) 751-8343 Fax: Call (573) 526-3669 for fax

MONTANA

Department of Justice
Motor Vehicle Division
Dealer Services Section
1003 Buckskin Dr.
Deer Lodge, MT 59722-2371
Phone: (406) 444-3661 Fax: (406) 846-6039

NEBRASKA

Motor Vehicle Industry Licensing Board
301 Centennial Mall South
P.O. Box 94697
Lincoln, NE 68509
Phone: (402) 471-2148 Fax: (402) 471-4563

NEVADA

Department of Motor Vehicles
Occupational and Business Licensing Section
555 Wright Way
Carson City, NV 89711
Phone: (775) 684-4690 Fax: (775) 684-4691

NEW HAMPSHIRE

New Hampshire Department of Safety
Division of Motor Vehicles Dealer & Inspection Desk
23 Hazen Dr.
Concord, NH 03305
Phone: (603) 271-2330 Fax: (603) 271-1061

NEW JERSEY

New Jersey Motor Vehicles Commission
Bureau of Business Licensing Services Unit
225 East State St., 2d Floor East
P.O. Box 171
Trenton, NJ 08666
Phone: (888) 486-3339 (toll-free in state)
Out of State: (609) 292-6500 (when prompted press 5013)
Fax: (609) 292-4400

NEW MEXICO

Motor Vehicle Division
Dealer Licensing Bureau
Joseph Montoya Building
P.O. Box 1028
1100 South St. Francis Drive
Sante Fe, NM 87504-1028
Phone: (888) 683-4636 Fax: (505) 841-6420

NEW YORK

FedEx Overnight Mailing Address:
New York State Department of Motor Vehicles
Vehicle Safety
ESP (Empire State Plaza)
Swann Street Building
Core 1, Room 110
Albany, NY 12228

Regular Mailing Address:
Bureau of Consumer and Facilities Services
Application Unit
P.O. Box 2700
Albany, NY 12220-0700

Physical Mailing Address:
Vehicle Safety Services
Application Unit
6 Empire State Plaza, Room 220
Albany, NY 12228-0001

Phone: (518) 474-0919 Fax: (518) 474-4702

NORTH CAROLINA

North Carolina Division of Motor Vehicles
Enforcement Section, Dealer Unit
3129 Mail Service Center
Raleigh, NC 27699-3129
Phone: (919) 861-3182 or (919) 715-7000
Fax: (919) 861-3805

NORTH DAKOTA

North Dakota Department of Transportation
Motor Vehicle Division
608 East Blvd.
Bismarck, ND 58505-0780
Phone: (701) 328-2725 (press 4) Fax: (701) 328-1487

OHIO

Mailing Address:
Bureau of Motor Vehicles
Dealer and Salesperson Licensing Unit
P.O. Box 16521
Columbus, OH 43216-6521
Phone: (614) 752-7636 Fax: (614) 752-7220

In Person:
Bureau of Motor Vehicles Customer Servicer Center (West)
1970 West Broad Street
Columbus, OH 43223-1101

OKLAHOMA

Oklahoma Motor Vehicle Commission
4334 N.W. Expressway, Suite 183
Oklahoma City, OK 73116-1515
Phone: (405) 607-8227 x101 Fax: (405) 607-8909

OREGON

Oregon Department of Transportation
Motor Vehicle Division
Business Licensing
1905 Lana Ave. N.E.
Salem, OR 97314
Phone: (503) 945-5052 Fax: (503) 945-5289

PENNSYLVANIA

[*Note: Complainants should contact both offices below.*]

Dealer Agent Services Group
Department of Transportation
Bureau of Motor Vehicles
1101 S. Front St.
Harrisburg, PA 17104
Phone: (717) 787-4291 Fax: (717) 787-9928

Pennsylvania State Board of Vehicle Manufacturers
Dealers and Salespersons
P.O. Box 2649
Harrisburg, PA 17105-2649
Phone: (717) 783-1697 Fax: (717) 787-0250

RHODE ISLAND

State of Rhode Island
Division of Motor Vehicles

Dealer Section
600 New London Ave.
Cranston, RI 02920-3024
Phone: (401) 462-4368 Fax: (401) 721-2697

SOUTH CAROLINA

Department of Motor Vehicles
Dealer License Section
P.O. Box 1498
Blythewood, SC 29016-0023
Phone: (803) 896-2611 or (803) 896-5000
Fax: (803) 896-2619

SOUTH DAKOTA

South Dakota Department of Revenue
Division of Motor Vehicles
Anderson Building
445 East Capitol Ave.
Pierre, SD 57501-3185
Phone: (605) 773-3541 Fax: (605) 773-2550

TENNESSEE

Tennessee Motor Vehicle Commission
500 James Robertson Parkway, 2nd Floor
Nashville, TN 37243-1153
Phone: (615) 741-2711 Fax: (615) 741-0651

TEXAS

Texas Department of Motor Vehicles
Motor Vehicle Division
Licensing Section
P.O. Box 2293
Austin, TX 78768
Phone: (888) 368-4689 or (877) 366-8887
Fax: (512) 302-2328

UTAH

Dealer Services
Utah State Tax Commission
Motor Vehicle Enforcement Division
210 North 1950 West
Salt Lake City, UT 84134
Phone: (801) 297-2600 Fax: (801) 297-2699

VERMONT

Vermont Motor Vehicle Department
Dealer Licensing

120 State St.
Montpelier, VT 05603
Phone: (802) 828-2038 Fax: (802) 828-2092

VIRGINIA

Motor Vehicle Dealer Board
Dealer Licensing Board
2201 West Broad St., Suite 104
Richmond, VA 23220
Phone: (804) 367-1100 Fax: (804) 367-1053

WASHINGTON

Washington Department of Licensing
Dealer & Manufacturer Services
P.O. Box 9034
Olympia, WA 98507
Phone: (360) 664-6466 or (360) 705-6744 (for application package)
Fax: (360) 586-6703

WEST VIRGINIA

First request for brochure of requirements address:
Office of Dealer Services
615 Washington St. East
Charleston, WV 25317
Phone: (304) 558-3584 Fax: (304) 558-1013

West Virginia Department of Transportation
Dealer Services
P.O. Box 17100
Charleston, WV 25317
Phone: (304) 926-0705 Fax: (304) 558-1013

WISCONSIN

Department of Transportation
Dealer and Agent Section
4802 Sheboygan Ave., Room 201
Madison, WI 53705
P.O. Box 7909
Madison, WI 53707-7909
Phone: (608) 266-1425 Fax: (608) 267-0323

WYOMING

Wyoming Department of Transportation
Dealer Licensing
5300 Bishop Blvd.
Cheyenne, WY 82009-3340
Phone: (307) 777-4717 Fax: (307) 777-4772

Appendix M	# Websites Related to Automobile Fraud

Page 653   ***Vehicle Title and Other History***

Replace "www.e-autohistory.com" with: www.experian.com/consumer-products/vehicle-history-report.html (Experian Auto History)

Page 654   ***Car Pricing Guides***

Replace "www.autoweb.com" with: www.autobytel.com

Replace "www.autosite.com" with: www.auto-site.com (AutoSite)

Finding Pleadings and Primary Sources on the Companion Website

N.1 Introduction

Automobile Fraud includes free access to its companion website, which remains free with continued subscription to this title. The companion website includes all appendices found in *Automobile Fraud* plus sample pleadings and dozens of other primary source documents—statutes, regulations, federal and state agency interpretations, and practice aids—all easily located with flexible, powerful search tools. Documents are available in Adobe Acrobat (PDF) format while pleadings are also available in Microsoft Word format.

This appendix describes the documents found on the companion website, how to access and print them, and how to download them to your computer or copy-paste excerpts into a word processing file. Note that the actual site may differ slightly in appearance from the screenshots below.

In addition to this appendix, we highly recommend reading the Help page on the website, found at the top of the left toolbar once you are logged in.

N.2 Pleadings and Primary Sources Found on the Companion Website

In addition to the current federal statutes and regulations relating to automobile fraud, the companion website to *Automobile Fraud* contains the federal Odometer Act prior to re-codification, key supplemental information to NHTSA regulations, summaries of state automobile fraud legislation, and NHTSA letters interpreting odometer requirements. Of particular note are over 100 sample pleadings for automobile fraud cases, including complaints, discovery requests, deposition transcripts, pre-trial motions, voir dire, opening statements, expert reports, closing statements, jury instructions, and attorney fee documents.

The website also has a number of tools to simplify title search requests, including applicable request forms from the 50 states, links to state titling offices, and sample reports from Carfax and other companies offering summary vehicle information.

The website does *not* contain the full text of this treatise's chapters. See Appx. N.6, *infra*, for instructions on how to use Internet-based keyword searches to pinpoint page numbers in the treatise where particular topics are discussed.

N.3 How to Access the Website

One-time registration is required to access the companion website. Once registered, a user subsequently logging in will be granted immediate access to all the companion websites he or she is authorized to use. For example, one username and password allows a subscriber to four NCLC titles to access all four related companion websites.

To register for the first time, go to **www.nclc.org/webaccess** and click the "Register as a New User" link. Enter the Companion Website Registration Number found on the packing statement or invoice accompanying this publication, then enter the requested information to create your account. An e-mail address may be used for the username, or a different username may be chosen.

Subscribers do *not* need to register more than once. If subscribers subsequently purchase additional NCLC titles, they will automatically be given access to the corresponding companion websites. Registering a second time with the same registration number overrides a prior username and password. (Note that if users allow all their subscriptions to lapse and then subsequently purchase a manual they must register again.)

Once registered, click on the log-in link at www.nclc.org/webaccess, enter the username and password, and select the *Automobile Fraud* website from the list of authorized websites.

An alternative log-in method may be particularly useful for libraries, legal aid offices, or law firms that subscribe to the entire set of NCLC treatises. Simply send an e-mail to publications@nclc.org with a list or range of static IP addresses for which access should be permitted. Users from those addresses can then go to www.nclc.org/ipaccess to be granted access *without* entering a username and password.

Once logged in, users can click the Preferences link located on the top toolbar to change their account information.

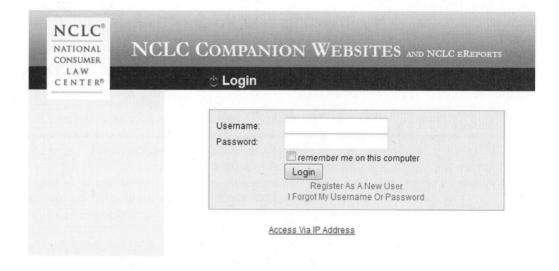

N.4 Locating Documents on the Website

The companion website provides three ways to locate documents:

1. The search page (the home page) uses keyword searches to find documents—full text searches of all documents on the website or searches of just the documents' titles. Enter text in the appropriate field and click the Search button.

- Narrow the search to documents of a certain type (for example, federal regulations or pleadings) by making a selection from the "Document Type" menu, and then perform a full text or document title search.
- To locate a specific appendix section, select the appendix section number (for example, A.2.3) or a partial identifier (for example, A) in the search page's "Appendix" drop-down fields.
- When searching documents' full text, each entry in your search results will include excerpts of the document, showing your search terms highlighted in context.
- Click on the "Search Hints" link for a quick reference to special search operators, wildcards, shortcuts, and complex searches. Read this information closely, as syntax and search operators may be slightly different from those used by other search engines.

2. The contents page (click the "Contents" tab at the top of the page) is a traditional nested table of contents. Click a branch to expand it into a list of sub-branches or documents. Each document appears once in this contents tree.

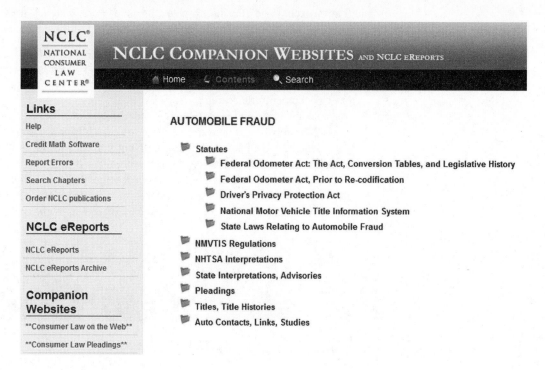

3. The pleading finder page (click the "Pleading Finder" link at the top of the search page) allows pleadings to be located using one or more menus (for example, "Type of Pleading—General" or "Subject"). For many users, this method will be the preferred way to find a pleading. More than one item can be selected from a menu by using the Ctrl key. For example, make one selection from "Type of Pleading—General," one from "Subject," and three from "Legal Claim" to locate all pleadings of that type and subject that contain one or more of the three legal claims selected. If this search produces insufficient results, deselect "Subject" or "Legal Claim" to find pleadings of that type in any subject area or based upon any legal claim.

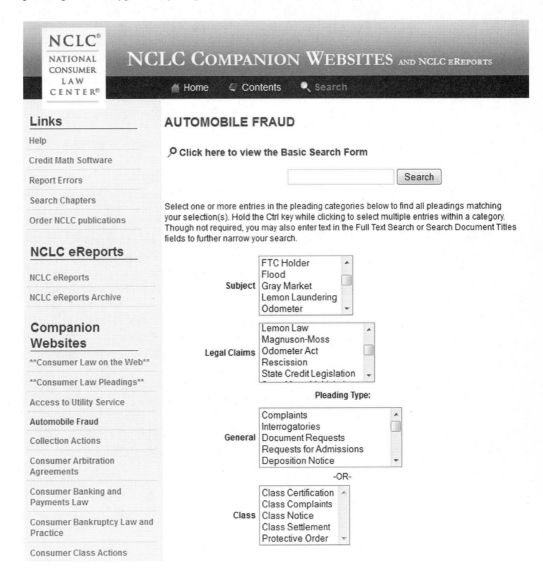

N.5 How to Use the Documents, Find Microsoft Word Versions, and Locate Additional Features

Click a document title in your search results or on the contents page to view the document in your web browser. Text may be copy-pasted directly from the page or the full document may be downloaded as a PDF file. (You will need a PDF reader to open PDF documents; the free Adobe Reader is available at www.adobe.com.) Additionally, pleadings and certain other documents can be downloaded in Microsoft Word format, enabling the opening of entire documents in a word processing program. Icons to download PDF and Word versions are found at the top of the page.

Links on the left toolbar bring you to credit math software, search tips, other websites, tables of contents and indices of all NCLC treatises, and other practice aids. Links to especially important new developments will be placed toward the bottom of the search page.

N.6 Electronic Searches of This and Other NCLC Titles' Chapters

Completely separate from the treatises' companion websites, NCLC offers a handy online utility to search the full text of this treatise's chapters and appendices. This free search utility is found at www.nclc.org/keyword and requires no registration or log-in.

While the chapters' text is not available online, this web-based search engine will find a word or phrase that can then easily be located in the printed treatise. Select *Automobile Fraud*, enter a search term or combination of search terms—such as a case name, a regulation citation, or other keywords—and the page numbers containing those terms will be listed. Search results are shown in context, enabling selection of the most relevant pages.

The full text of other NCLC treatises, supplements, and other publications can also be searched to locate relevant topics at www.nclc.org/keyword. Just select the desired title or search all NCLC titles.

Current tables of contents, indices, and other information for all twenty titles in the NCLC *Consumer Credit and Sales Legal Practice Series* can be found at www.nclc.org/shop. Click the "For Lawyers" link and scroll down to the book you are interested in. The PDF-format documents found there can be quickly searched for a word or phrase.

The Quick Reference, found at www.nclc.org/qr, is an alphabetical index spanning all twenty NCLC treatises. It lists over 1000 subjects and indicates the book(s) and section(s) where each subject is discussed.

N.7 Finding Additional Pleadings

Pleadings specifically relating to this title are found in Adobe Acrobat (PDF) and Microsoft Word format on the companion website. Over 2000 other pleadings are available in NCLC's *Consumer Law Pleadings* and can be found on the *Consumer Law Pleadings* companion website using the same search techniques discussed above. These 2000 pleadings can also be located using the *Consumer Law Pleadings* index guide, which organizes pleadings by type, subject area, legal claim, title, and other categories identical to those used on the website.

State Statutes and Regulations Relating to Yo-Yo Sales

This appendix summarizes state states and regulations relating to yo-yo sales, including those that require retail installment contracts to include all essential terms.

ALASKA

Alaska Stat. § 45.25.610

Prohibited acts: Noncompliance with required procedures and notices.

Required procedures: For a sale contract contingent on seller obtaining financing, dealer must provide the specified disclosures signed by buyer prior to delivery of the vehicle. Upon return of vehicle following cancellation, dealer must provide full return of any consideration received from buyer, including trade-in, less any amount due dealer for usage over 100 miles or damage to, or charges for, vehicle while in buyer's possession. Dealer is to provide, in addition to installment contract, a separate agreement as to buyer rights while financial approval is being obtained. Trade-in to be returned in same condition and with less than 100 miles usage by dealer.

Required notices: Contingent sales document to include conspicuously and clearly specified information as to final payment arrangements, notice that acceptance of delivery obligates buyer to terms of contract if terms unchanged upon approval of financing, and notice that contract is void if any terms are changed by dealer or the financing institution as a condition for finalizing sale.

Enforcement: None specified.

ARIZONA

Ariz. Rev. Stat. Ann. §§ 44-1371 (sales and leases), 44-286

Prohibited acts: When sale or lease conditioned on final approval of financing, the sale or lease of trade-in vehicle prohibited prior to final approval or prior to return to buyer (§ 44-1371). Sale contract to have no blank spaces (§ 44-286).

Required procedures: Until financing for sale or lease is approved or disapproved, seller must retain title to, and possession of, trade-in vehicle.

Required notices: In 10-point boldface type, notice to buyer not to sign if contract has blank spaces, and that buyer has right to copy of completed contract (§ 44-286).

Enforcement: Any remedy for violation may not be waived, modified, or limited by agreement. Violation of § 44-286 bars recovery of contractual charges (Ariz. Rev. Stat. Ann. § 44-295).

CALIFORNIA

Cal. Civ. Code § 2982.5 (West)

Prohibited acts: Seller may not provide any security or other guaranty of payment on loan made to buyer, and may not receive any commission or other remuneration for assisting the buyer to obtain the loan.

Required procedures: If the buyer obligates himself or herself to purchase, or receives possession of, the motor vehicle prior to securing loan, and if the buyer upon appropriate application for loan is unable to secure loan, on the conditions stated in the conditional sale contract, the conditional sale contract or purchase order shall be deemed rescinded and all consideration thereupon shall be returned by the respective parties without demand.

Required notices: If the buyer becomes obligated to purchase, or receives possession of, the motor vehicle prior to obtaining loan, the agreement shall state, *inter alia*, the amount of the loan, the finance charge, the number and amount of the installment payments, and must include a notice to the buyer in at least 8-point type that the buyer is obligated for the installment payments on the loan and for any payments which may be due on the agreement between the buyer and the seller. Seller may not receive any commission or other remuneration for assisting buyer to obtain loan. If buyer upon proper application for loan is unable to obtain loan, on the condition stated in the agreement between buyer and seller, the agreement shall be deemed rescinded and all consideration thereunder shall be returned by the respective parties without demand.

Enforcement: Violation is misdemeanor (Cal. Civ. Code § 1983.6 (West)). Violation is probably actionable by consumers as a violation of state's Unfair Competition Law.

COLORADO

Colo. Rev. Stat. § 6-1-708 (sales and leases)

Prohibited acts: Deceptive business practice to: (1) guarantee, as defined, approval of sale or lease when sale contract or lease conditioned on credit approval; (2) sell or lease trade-in vehicle before transaction finalized; (3) fail to return any collateral or down payment tendered pending credit approval when financing not approved.

Required procedures: Upon rejection of credit application, seller must return any and all down payments including trade-in vehicle; retention of any part as payment for rent of released vehicle is unlawful, even when buyer and dealer agree to waiver or to a rental agreement.

Required notices: None specified.

Enforcement: The buyer may seek damages for deceptive trade practices violation (Colo. Rev. Stat. § 6-1-113).

DELAWARE

Del. Code Ann. tit. 5, § 2907(a), (c), (i)

Prohibited acts: Noncompliance with sale contract requirements.

Required procedures: Sale contract to have no blank spaces and contain essential financial details as specified. Some blank spaces as to vehicle identification and date of first installment may be left blank if vehicle not yet delivered to buyer. Prior to delivery of required contract to buyer, buyer may rescind contract and receive complete refund of any down payment including trade-in.

Required notices: In 10-point boldface type, notice to buyer not to sign if contract has blank spaces, and that buyer has right to copy of completed contract.

Enforcement: Fines and forfeiture of fees and charges (Del. Code Ann. tit. 5, § 2911).

FLORIDA

Fla. Stat. § 520.07

Prohibited acts: Noncompliance with sale contract requirements.

Required procedures: Sale contract to have no blank spaces and contain essential financial details as specified. Some blank spaces as to vehicle identification and date of first installment may be left blank if vehicle not yet delivered to buyer. Prior to delivery of required contract to buyer, buyer may rescind contract and receive complete refund of any down payment including trade-in.

Required notices: Notice to buyer not to sign if contract has blank spaces, and that buyer has right to copy of completed contract.

Enforcement: Violation punishable as first degree misdemeanor; revocation or suspension of dealer license. Unless buyer received copy of the complete contract as required, buyer may recover fees and charges, plus costs and attorney fees (Fla. Stat. §§ 520.12, 520.995).

GEORGIA

Ga. Code Ann. § 10-1-32

Prohibited acts: Noncompliance with sale contract requirements.

Required procedures: Sale contract to have no blank spaces; however, no specific financial arrangements are included as required elements of contract. Some blank spaces as to vehicle identification and date of first installment may be left blank if vehicle not yet delivered to buyer. Prior to delivery of required contract to buyer, buyer may rescind contract and receive complete refund of any down payment including trade-in.

Required notices: Notice to buyer not to sign if contract has blank spaces, and that buyer has right to copy of completed contract.

Enforcement: Violation punishable as misdemeanor; fine; violation bars recovery of contractual charges. If violation willful, buyer may recover damages, costs, and attorney fees (Ga. Code Ann. § 10-1-38).

IDAHO

Idaho Admin. Code r. 04.02.01.237

Prohibited acts: If sale becomes null and void, dealer must return trade-in vehicle upon buyer's return of the purchased vehicle; if trade-in vehicle is no longer available, dealer must pay consumer the trade-in allowance within one business day.

Required procedures: None specified.

Required notices: Disclosure that buyer has agreed that vehicle will be delivered prior to the purchase, and that contract will be null and void if financing cannot be arranged on the same terms and within the time period agreed upon.

Enforcement: Rule adopted under state UDAP statute, Idaho Code Ann. § 48-608, which provides a private right of action for actual damages or $1000, whichever is greater, punitive damages in court's discretion, attorney fees, and various other relief.

ILLINOIS

815 Ill. Comp. Stat. § 505/2C

Prohibited acts: Failure to return down payment, including trade-in, if furnishing of merchandise, whether under purchase order or contract of sale, is conditioned on consumer providing credit references or having a credit rating acceptable to seller and seller rejects the consumer's credit application.

Required procedures: None specified.
Required notices: None specified.
Enforcement: This prohibition is part of the state UDAP statute and buyer may seek damages and attorney fees (815 Ill. Comp. Stat. § 505/10a). State's attorney may seek civil damages and injunction (815 Ill. Comp. Stat. § 505/7).

LOUISIANA

La. Rev. Stat. Ann. § 32:1261(2)(f)

Prohibited acts: Noncompliance with required procedures and notices.

Required procedures: Dealer must provide buyer with written notice of terms of "spot delivery," a conditional sale contract signed by buyer. Dealer not to sell trade-in until sale finalized.

Required notices: Contingent sale contract to include specified information including: time limits; what fees are authorized; trade-in not to be sold until sale finalized; upon non-completion of sale, the right to immediate refund and requirements as to buyer's return of vehicle.

Enforcement: The Motor Vehicle Commission may seek injunction; assess civil penalty; or revoke, suspend, or fail to renew dealer license (La. Rev. Stat. Ann. §§ 32:1258 to 32:1260).

MASSACHUSETTS

940 Mass. Code Regs. § 5.04

Prohibited acts: Failure to return buyer's deposit promptly when buyer cancels before contract has been accepted by authorized dealer representative, or when contract is subject to buyer's ability to obtain financing of his or her choice and the buyer cannot obtain financing after reasonable efforts. Seller must not increase purchase price after accepting buyer's purchase offer; trade-in value may be reappraised only if evidence found of substitution or damage prior to transfer to seller.

Required procedures: None specified.

Required notices: Contract must specify any conditions precedent and must state that buyer may cancel purchase offer until dealer accepts it.

Enforcement: Violations are UDAP violations.

MISSISSIPPI

Miss. Code Ann. § 63-19-31

Prohibited acts: Noncompliance with sale contract requirements.

Required procedures: Sale contract to have no blank spaces and contain all essential financial details as specified. Some blank spaces as to vehicle identification and date of first installment may be left blank if vehicle not yet delivered to buyer. Prior to delivery of required contract to buyer, buyer may rescind contract and receive complete refund of any down payment including trade-in.

Required notices: In 10-point boldface type, notice to buyer not to sign if contract has blank spaces, and that buyer has right to copy of completed contract.

Enforcement: Willful violation a misdemeanor; commissioner of Banking and Consumer Finance may levy fines for violations and also may seek injunctive relief; willful violation is bar to recovery of contractual charges (Miss. Code Ann. § 63-19-55).

MISSOURI

Mo. Rev. Stat. § 365.070

Prohibited acts: Noncompliance with sale contract requirements.

Required procedures: Sale contract to have no blank spaces and contain all essential financial details as specified. Prior to delivery of required contract to buyer, buyer may rescind contract and receive complete refund of any down payment including trade-in.

Required notices: In 10-point boldface type, notice to buyer not to sign if contract has blank spaces, and that buyer has right to copy of completed contract.

Enforcement: Knowing violation punishable as class B misdemeanor; violation bars recovery of contractual charges (Mo. Rev. Stat. § 365.150).

NEVADA

Nev. Rev. Stat. § 482.554

Prohibited acts: A seller who enters into a vehicle sale contract on credit, exercises a valid option to cancel the vehicle sale, and then, after the customer returns the vehicle with no damage other than reasonable wear and tear, falsely represents that buyer must sign another sale contract on less favorable terms, or then fails to return trade-in or any other consideration in full, or then fails to supply the required disclosure prior to entering into a new agreement.

Required procedures: None specified.

Required notices: Prior to entering a new agreement after canceling original sale, seller must provide buyer with disclosure form provided by Department of Public Safety (Nev. Admin. Code § 482.935).

Enforcement: The Department of Public Safety may assess administrative fine up to $10,000 (§ 482.554(1)); or seek injunction (Nev. Rev. Stat. § 482.565). Administrative remedy is in addition to any other legal remedy available to victim of deceptive practices (§ 482.554(3)).

NEW HAMPSHIRE

N.H. Rev. Stat. Ann. §§ 361-A:7, 361-A:10-b

Prohibited acts: Noncompliance with required procedures and notices.

Required procedures: Sale contract to have no blank spaces and contain all essential financial details as specified; some blank spaces as to vehicle identification and date of first installment may be left blank if vehicle not yet delivered to buyer (§ 361-A:7). For a sale contract contingent on seller obtaining financing, dealer must provide the specified disclosure signed by buyer upon delivery of the vehicle. Upon return of vehicle following cancellation, dealer must provide full return of any consideration received from buyer.

Required notices: Details of specified disclosure, in 10-point boldface type, include notice to buyer not to sign if contract has blank spaces, that buyer has right to copy of completed contract, notice of the cancellation of sale if seller unable to obtain financing, followed by the buyer returning vehicle and receiving any consideration received by seller including any trade-in.

Enforcement: Violation may lead to administrative fine, injunction, and revocation or suspension of dealer license (N.H. Rev. Stat. Ann. § 361-A:11).

NEW MEXICO

N.M. Stat. Ann. § 58-19-7

Prohibited acts: Noncompliance with sale contract requirements.

Required procedures: No party to sign any sale contract having blank spaces; sale contract must contain essential financial details as specified. Some blank spaces as to vehicle identification and date of first installment may be left blank if vehicle not yet delivered to buyer. Prior to delivery of required contract to buyer, buyer may rescind contract and receive complete refund of any down payment including trade-in.

Required notices: In 10-point boldface type, notice to buyer not to sign if contract has blank spaces, and that buyer has right to copy of completed contract.

Enforcement: Willful violation is misdemeanor resulting in fine; willful violation bars recovery of contractual charges (N.M. Stat. Ann. § 58-19-11).

NEW YORK

N.Y. Pers. Prop. Law § 302 (McKinney)

Prohibited acts: Noncompliance with sale contract requirements.

Required procedures: No party to sign sale contract having blank spaces and all information required by federal Truth in Lending Act. Some blank spaces as to vehicle identification and date of first installment may be left blank if vehicle not yet delivered to buyer. Prior to delivery of required contract to buyer, buyer may rescind contract and receive complete refund of any down payment including trade-in.

Required notices: Include, in 10-point boldface type, notice to buyer not to sign if contract has blank spaces, and that buyer has right to copy of completed contract.

Enforcement: Willful violation is misdemeanor resulting in fine; willful violation bars recovery of contractual charges (N.Y. Pers. Prop. Law § 307 (McKinney)).

NORTH CAROLINA

N.C. Gen. Stat. § 20-75.1

Prohibited acts: None. Provides that other sections of North Carolina statutes do not prohibit a dealer from entering into a contract with any purchaser for sale of a vehicle and delivering the vehicle to the purchaser under terms by which the dealer's obligation to execute the manufacturer's certificate of origin or the certificate of title is conditioned on the purchaser obtaining financing for the purchase of the vehicle. Regulates insurance coverage for yo-yo sales.

Required procedures: None specified.

Required notices: None.

Enforcement: None specified.

NORTH DAKOTA

N.D. Cent. Code § 51-13-02

Prohibited acts: Noncompliance with sale contract requirements.

Required procedures: Sale contract to have no blank spaces and contain essential financial details as specified. Some blank spaces as to vehicle identification and date of first installment may be left blank if vehicle not yet delivered to buyer. Prior to delivery of required contract to buyer, buyer may rescind contract and receive complete refund of any down payment including trade-in.

Required notices: Include, in 10-point boldface type, notice to buyer not to sign if contract has blank spaces, and that buyer has right to copy of completed contract.

Enforcement: Willful violation is misdemeanor resulting in fine; willful violation bars recovery of contractual charges (N.D. Cent. Code § 51-13-07).

OHIO

Ohio Admin Code 109:4-3-16(B)(30)

Prohibited acts: Deliver a motor vehicle to a consumer pursuant to a sale which is contingent upon financing without a written agreement stating the parties' obligations should such financing not be obtained.

Required procedures: Provide written agreement as to parties' obligations should financing not be obtained.

Required notices: None specified.

Enforcement: Violation is a deceptive act or practice.

OREGON

Or. Rev. Stat. § 646A.090

Prohibited acts: Seller may make an offer to sell or lease a motor vehicle to buyer or prospective buyer that is subject to future acceptance by lender that may finance the transaction at request of seller. If lender does not agree to finance the transaction on the exact terms negotiated between buyer and seller within fourteen days after the date on which buyer takes possession of motor vehicle, seller must return all items of value to buyer, unless buyer fails to return vehicle upon notification from seller. Seller may not sell or lease buyer's trade-in vehicle until seller has obtained final approval from lender. Buyer and seller may agree that buyer will be responsible for excessive wear and tear on vehicle and a reasonable mileage charge.

Required procedures: None specified.

Required notices: None specified.

Enforcement: Violation is a deceptive act or practice.

PENNSYLVANIA

63 Pa. Stat. Ann. §§ 818.2, 818.19 (West); 37 Pa. Code § 301.4

Prohibited acts: "Bushing," defined as the practice of increasing vehicle's selling price above that originally quoted the purchaser or decreasing the allowance for trade-in after buyer signs a purchase order or contract subject to subsequent acceptance by seller (§ 818.2); *see also* 37 Pa. Code § 301.4(a)(7), (8) (prohibiting increasing vehicle price or decreasing trade-in allowance).

Required procedures: Dealer must provide buyer with copies of sale documents and required notices (37 Pa. Code § 301.4).

Required notices: Sale contract to include specified information including a list of conditions precedent to the dealer's acceptance of the contract, set forth in a clear and conspicuous manner, as well as a statement that purchaser may cancel contract at any time until the conditions are met (37 Pa. Code § 301.4(a)(2)(v)).

Enforcement: The State Board of Vehicle Manufacturers, Dealers and Salespersons may seek injunction, assess civil penalty (63 Pa. Stat. Ann. § 818.28 (West)), or revoke, suspend, or fail to renew dealer license (§ 818.19(36)). Buyer may seek damages or injunction (63 Pa. Stat. Ann. § 818.29 (West)). Regulation (37 Pa. Code § 301.4) was adopted under state UDAP statute and thus violation is a UDAP violation.

TEXAS

Tex. Fin. Code Ann. § 348.013 (West)

Prohibited acts: Failure to return trade-in and down payment (or trade-in's stated cash value if it cannot be returned in same or substantially same condition) upon failure to convert conditional delivery agreement to retail installment contract.

Required procedures: Conditional delivery agreement is an enforceable contract but may not exceed term of 15 days. It does not confer any legal or equitable rights of ownership.

Required notices: Conditional delivery agreement must state agreed value of trade-in vehicle.

Enforcement: The Consumer Credit Commissioner may order retail seller to pay value of trade-in vehicle to consumer and may impose administrative penalty; an administrative appeal procedure is provided. The statute provides that it does not create a private cause of action. *See also* Tex. Fin. Code Ann. § 353.015 (West) (similar provisions when vehicle is sold for other than personal, family, or household use).

UTAH

Utah Code Ann. §§ 41-3-401, 41-3-401.5 (leases) (West)

Prohibited acts: Failure to provide notices or comply with procedures as required.

Required procedures: On front page of sale contract contingent on financing dealer must provide required notice prior to releasing possession of vehicle, and subsequently must act within prescribed time limits. Full refund to buyer required if vehicle returned upon rescission.

Required notices: Specified language of disclosure form includes time limits for buyer and seller if initial arrangement is canceled; return of trade-in or sum equivalent of trade-in, with any other consideration, upon buyer's return of vehicle.

Enforcement: Buyer may seek damages (Utah Code Ann. § 41-3-404 (West)). Buyer may rescind sale contract for full refund. Violation by dealer is misdemeanor.

VERMONT

Vt. Stat. Ann. tit. 9, § 2355

Prohibited acts: Noncompliance with sale contract requirements.

Required procedures: Sale contract to have no blank spaces and contain essential financial details as specified. Some blank spaces as to vehicle identification and date of first installment may be left blank if vehicle not yet delivered to buyer. Prior to delivery of required contract to buyer, buyer may rescind contract and receive complete refund of any down payment including trade-in.

Required notices: In 10-point boldface type, notice to buyer not to sign if contract has blank spaces, and that buyer has right to copy of completed contract.

Enforcement: Fines; buyer has right to action for real and punitive damages, costs, and attorney fees (Vt. Stat. Ann. tit. 9, § 2361).

VIRGINIA

Va. Code Ann. § 46.2-1530

Prohibited acts: Noncompliance with required procedures and notices.

Required procedures: Dealer must complete two buyer order forms, the original to be kept for five years, the duplicate to be provided to buyer during negotiation and prior to sale. A sample buyer order form including statement of any processing fee is to be filed with state Motor Vehicle Dealer Board with dealer licensing application.

Required notices: Order form to include specified information including sale price, amount of cash deposit, trade-in description (if any), amounts of individually identified fees and taxes, net balance due at settlement, notice of buyer liability and rights in boldface type, and notice whether liability insurance is included in 18-point type. Processing fees, if any, to be posted conspicuously in sales area.

Enforcement: The Motor Vehicle Dealer Board may seek injunction, assess civil penalty, or revoke, suspend or fail to renew dealer license (Va. Code Ann. §§ 46.2-1530.4, 46.2-1505, 46.2-1507).

WASHINGTON

Wash. Rev. Code §§ 46.70.180(4) (sales and leases), 63.14.070

Prohibited acts: "Bushing," defined as the practice of agreeing to sale contract or lease when: (1) dealer has right to rescind, and when dealer fails within four weekdays to inform buyer or lessee of dealer's unconditionally accepting or rejecting lease or sale contract, and (2) when such contract permits dealer to renegotiate value of trade-in except for substantial changes discovered in condition of trade-in. Obtaining buyer's signature on contract that contains blank spaces as to essential provisions (§ 63.14.070).

Required procedures: Dealer must notify buyer within four weekdays as to whether contract accepted or rejected by dealer. If rejected, dealer must tender full refund including return of trade-in; tender may be contingent upon return of vehicle subject to sale.

Required notices: If communication to buyer of acceptance or rejection is by e-mail, another means of communication must also be used.

Enforcement: The buyer may seek damages, costs, and attorney fees within one year of violation (Wash. Rev. Code § 46.70.190). State director of licensing may refer information about violation to attorney general for purpose of seeking injunction or, within six years of violation, seeking damages (Wash. Rev. Code § 46.70.220).

WISCONSIN

Wis. Stat. § 218.0116(1)(im) (sales and leases)

Prohibited acts: "Bushing," defined as the practice of increasing vehicle's selling price above that originally quoted purchaser as evidenced by a purchase order or contract signed by seller and buyer. For leases, an increase in the gross capitalized cost above that originally quoted the lessee as evidenced by a consumer lease or prelease agreement signed by lessee and dealer.

Required procedures: None specified.

Required notices: None specified.

Enforcement: State Department of Transportation may revoke, suspend, or fail to renew dealer license.

Index and Quick Reference

Quick Reference to the Consumer Law Practice Series

The Quick Reference to the Consumer Law Practice Series pinpoints where to find specific topics analyzed in any of the nineteen NCLC treatises. The Quick Reference is now available at www.nclc.org/qr. Placing the Quick Reference on a website ensures that readers have the most up-to-date version, including any revised section numbering.

Another way to locate topics is to go to www.nclc.org/keyword and perform keyword searches on individual treatises or across all NCLC publications. This function allows for compound searches such as "identity theft (near) punitive damages," and shows results in context, with the appropriate book title and page number where the reference is found.

Pleadings related just to *Automobile Fraud* can be found on the companion website to this title, and can be located using different search functions, including the "Pleading Finder." For more information, see page ix, *supra*.

NCLC also has over 2000 additional sample pleadings on websites accompanying our other titles. The best way to locate and access a pleading among this broader group is to use NCLC's *Consumer Law Pleadings Index Guide* or the finding aids on its website.

More information on individual treatises in this series is available in What Your Library Should Contain, page v, *supra*, or by going to www.nclc.org/shop. A more detailed index for *Automobile Fraud* is found at the back of this treatise's main volume and supplemented below.

Supplement Index

The Index for *Automobile Fraud* is found at the back of this treatise's main volume. Additional changes to that Index, including new topics found only in this Supplement, are found below. References are to sections; references followed by "S" appear only in this Supplement.